$MONEY

-BY THE

MOUTHFUL!

By Robert O. Nara D.D.S.
WITH STEVEN ALEXANDER MARINER

ORAMEDICS INTERNATIONAL PRESS
International Standard Book No.
0-933420

WHAT YOU SHOULD KNOW ABOUT THE HEALTH OF YOUR MOUTH & BODY...

THAT NO DOCTOR IS GOING TO TELL YOU...

First Printing — January 1979
Second Printing — September 1979

Library of Congress Catalogue
79-91111

International Standard Book No.
0-933420-00-5

CONTENTS

Please note

For your convenience we have included several note pages in the back of this book.

As you read this book please make notes of your thoughts, feelings, questions, or comments.

The pages are labeled "notes to myself" which speaks for itself. However, you may include any comments to relate to the authors and/or your personal dentist.

Foreword by Steven A. Mariner

My initial reluctance to become associated with Doctor Robert Nara and Oramedics International, which he founded, was probably for the same reasons many will at first doubt what they are about to read.

To begin with, I had believed common knowledge all my life: That there was no hope for my teeth, that they'd get sick and eventually fall out or be pulled out and replaced with dentures. I was not prepared by anything I had heard or read for the mind-altering truth that *all dental disease is wholly preventable —today.*

My second objection to becoming involved was that I assumed Doctor Nara was one of those lunatics found on the fringes of every profession; a man bent upon establishing his own empire or attacking The Establishment simply because he had nothing better to do.

How wrong I was. Doctor Nara's credentials fill eleven closely-spaced, typed pages; he is profoundly competent to tell this story from any viewpoint: Education, experience, honors and awards; personal, financial and professional success. He is a true visionary and leader in an age —and profession —in which leadership is sadly lacking.

What Doctor Nara is telling the world about oral health is, if true, the most shocking health scandal in this country. This book will offer proofs; the reader will ultimately have to judge. Other judges in courts and government agencies are, today, facing the same decision.

If true, this story tells of multi-billion-dollar waste every year. It tells of huge companies manufacturing and advertising products which you not only don't need; they are actually gravely, seriously bad for your health.

You will read about dentists whose license allows them to accept large fees, from you, for doing things that will cause you more sickness. You will discover that the disfigurement, the pain, the expense and futility of conventional dentistry —in *your* life —could have been and should have been avoided...all of it.

You will learn how dental disease actually works, and why conventional dentistry is all but helpless to do anything about it —even though they know how.

You will find that the dentist who most wants to help you is legally prevented from telling you about his service. You will read about the nearly unbelievable lengths conventional dentistry will go to to keep this information from the public, and to punish dentists who insist on telling the truth.

Most importantly, though: You'll learn in this book how *you* can take advantage of what dentists and doctors know, and won't tell you; information that can show you how to simply and economically —and forever —achieve freedom from dental disease.

Before Doctor Nara convinced me of these things, I was unwilling to share authorship in this book. Now, however, this writing transcends simply something a writer does for a living. It has become a mission of sorts, because I am angry —as is almost everyone who becomes aware of the magnitude of this scandal. Hopefully, you too will become indignant and angry. Why?

—Because something has to be done about these things. Since the dental profession itself refuses to accept its responsibility, it's up to the people. In America, the people ultimately make all the important decisions and demand progress. It's up to you, now...

Chapter One:
"Let's Get Honest"

Before anyone can hope to learn the truth about oral health and about America's most shocking public health scandal, we must get rid of several mis-truths, half-truths and outright lies. Together, these things make up the public's "common knowledge" about this subject. Every one of us views the world through what is sometimes called "frames of reference." In other words, we hear and see and understand based on previously established information.

The frame of reference, then, is sort of a foundation upon which we continue to build our house of knowledge on any given subject. If the foundation is bad, the knowledge will be defective no matter how well-constructed it appears to be.

The public frame of reference to oral health, teeth, dental disease and dentistry is a foundation built on quicksand. No other aspect of health today suffers from so many misconceptions and professional deceptions.

First, and most important: Teeth are meant to last your whole lifetime. No other part of your body is as tough, as well-constructed and capable of recovering from disease. Given half a chance, your mouth would be —and should be —the healthiest part of you, forever.

It is "common knowledge" that teeth will get cavities while young and need to be replaced when old. This is worse than a misconception: It's an outright lie. In the absence of dental disease none of these things happen to teeth —which brings us to public misconception number two:

"There's nothing anyone can do about dental disease." How many times have you heard that? TV advertising, for example, makes a virtue out of *minimizing* disease, not doing away with it. Later in this book you will discover the causes of disease and how to prevent it. For now, let's just do away with the belief that dental problems are inevitable and replace that with the truth: There is no longer any reason for anyone to have bad oral health. The disease doesn't have to be feared; just eliminated.

Another incredibly damaging misconception is that dentures are an acceptable replacement for natural teeth. False teeth are one of the most lucrative tricks in the dentist's bag, but they are dangerous to your health. More about this in another chapter; for now, however: Dentures can cost you up to ten years right off the top of an otherwise normal lifetime. Aside from cosmetic problems and a host of mental problems; aside from the inconvenience and expense and actual decrease of longevity, dentures will rob you of physical health and vitality for the balance of your life. People think of dentures as "not bad." They *should* think of dentures as poison.

People are taught to think of proper care (when they think of it at all) as being something like this: "Brush after meals, use floss, avoid sweets and see the dentist every six months." Later you'll discover that formula to be virtually useless; people whose health depends upon it, and who use it as a guide, are fooling themselves.

We are told, or assume, that cavities are caused by sugar. That's a lie. Cavities are caused by *disease,* and the disease is caused by germs. You can avoid sugar all you wish but you will not escape dental disease because of your abstinence.

Let's take a second glance at the preceding paragraph. It says, "...disease is caused by germs." *Is that true?* —It sure is! In another chapter we will go through the disease mechanism step-by-step, and you can understand, then, not only how the germs do their dirty work, but exactly which germs are guilty...and how to get rid of them.

If that seems familiar to you, it's probably because you are familiar with germs and disease processes elsewhere in your body. When you think about it (when

2

the misconceptions are gotten out of the way), it seems simply obvious that oral health would not be too much different from physical health. Excellent conclusion! You are already beginning to uncover the truth.

Are you ready for this: Disease-free teeth which have been damaged by former disease *can heal themselves.* If that surprised you, think about the preceding paragraph again. Oral health, logically and reasonably, has many parallels with physical health. Broken bones knit; damaged hearts heal, torn muscles or cut skin mends...the body's ability to heal is the *norm,* not the exception. Why should the mouth be different? —It isn't.

For many reasons —mostly because of our gigantic misconception about oral health —this aspect of our overall health is not considered important by most of us. It should be. Aside from basic nutritional balance, which has its origin in a healthy mouth and affects the whole body, we should know that oral health is responsible for an amazing share of our "whole" health.

Oral health can be a matter of life or death for diabetics, hemophiliacs, and others. Your oral health can protect you from a host of frightening things such as hepatitis or even venereal disease. Bad oral health is a gateway for diseases elsewhere in the body, including but in no way limited to the two just mentioned.

By now you may be wondering why this information isn't more widely discussed. If public knowledge is so flagrantly incorrect, why isn't it corrected?

The question is this: Who would do the correcting? If the establishment of professional dentistry doesn't do it, how will it get done? And that is one of the most startling, scandalous parts of what you are going to discover. Conventional dentistry has abdicated its responsibility as healers and doctors; has traded its honor for a fat bank account. Dentistry today doesn't want you to prevent dental disease because there is too much income to be had repairing disease-damaged teeth. The profession teaches and performs services designed to repair or replace symptoms; the dentist does nothing to attack the disease itself.

Professional dentists don't even have a name for dental disease. They have classified all of the symptoms, but there has been so little interest in the disease itself they haven't bothered to name it. They simply call it "dental disease," with the implication that there is nothing to be done about it.

It is, today, a violation of dental professional ethics —and of most state laws —to advertise to the public that a dentist is interested in preventing disease and its problems. Dentists *can* advertise various specialties (when recognized by the association), but these all deal with repair of damages. The association which makes and enforces the rules has adamantly refused to sanction preventive (medical) dentistry as a specialty, even though medical doctors have long considered prevention one of the more ideal forms of health care and treatment.

Throughout this book you will read about discoveries made by Oramedics International and about methods used by dentists who are practicing Oramedics Fellows. In no way should this be interpreted that the book is trying to "sell" Oramedics, either to the public or to the profession.

Preventive medical dentistry is the sole hope of our national oral health disgrace. Oramedics International has preventive medical dentistry —disease prevention —as its single purpose. Oramedics does not pretend to be the only path to oral health, nor is its attitude that Oramedics International has some corner on preventive knowledge.

Oramedics International is, however, the most visible vehicle for this "new" information and is, as far as can be determined, the only agency in this country still willing to withstand the court battles, the incredible organized resistance, the discouragement and punishment met by anyone who espouses these ideas.

4

Others have tried, and have been slapped down. If this truth is to reach the people —and, for our health's sake, it must reach the people —Oramedics is today the most logical and viable method of carrying the message. If any others follow after with different names, different concepts; but with prevention of dental disease as their central theme, they are more than welcome.

Finally: You will see forms and charts used by Oramedics Fellows; there will be patient testimonies and Oramedics statistics, we will discuss Oramedics laboratory testing and procedures.

These are not meant to advertise the "Oramedics Way," as if there was some magic in the name. Instead, we use these things because they are, today, perhaps the only valid proofs that we can eliminate dental disease in this generation, if we want to.

There will be many detractors: This book is not going to be appreciated by conventional organized dentistry. Therefore, let's conclude this chapter on eliminating mis-truths and half-truths by mentioning something about the organization which will attempt to discredit what you're about to read.

People (organized dentistry) who disagree with this would have us believe that America's dental/oral health is in good hands. The U.S. Health Department says that 98 out of 100 Americans are suffering from dental disease.

Somebody isn't telling the truth...

Chapter Two
The Truth About Dental Disease

If somebody asked you to peel a fruit, you'd probably cheerfully agree to the chore. What if you were then handed a tomato? You'd have to stop and think, wouldn't you? First of all —is a tomato really a fruit, or is it a vegetable? Next: How do you go about peeling a tomato? Do you have to cook it first? Why peel it at all; isn't it better just sliced or quartered or stewed, peel and all?

Obviously what happened is that you were invited to do something your frame of reference was comfortable with: Peeling fruit; and you were comfortable because you immediately thought of apples, oranges, tangerines —all of the fruits you were familiar with in the context of being peeled. And then, suddenly, the frame of reference was confused or shattered when you were confronted with the unexpected, the unusual; the different.

The purpose of this little exercise is to provoke your thinking about something you believe you are familiar with —but which, in reality, will suddenly become totally unfamiliar. Most people have a tendency to ignore or even slightly fear the unknown and unfamiliar. This very human trait is partially responsible for the gross misconceptions most people have concerning dental disease.

Remember: Even though this book will tell you many things about dentistry in general and about the state of America's dental health that will be "scary" the main message is *good news*. With that encouragement, get ready to plunge into the unknown; discard your old, familiar concepts and misconceptions: Bring your newly opened curiosity to the truth about dental disease.

Welcome to the world of *Odontosis*. Do you recall in Chapter One when you learned that professional dentistry has no name for dental disease? That's true;

6

and it was a defect in our knowledge that had to be corrected. Oramedics, therefore, assigned the name "odontosis" to replace the mysterious title "dental disease." We don't call pneumonia "lung disease," nor do we call diptheria "throat disease" —and on, and on. As we learn how men's enemies —diseases —are caused, and how to cure them or prevent them, we replace the mystery with a name. Dental disease is no longer a mysterious malady: It is a preventable disease Oramedics calls "odontosis."

There are three members of the odontosis family; three more-or-less recognizable progressions of what is in reality the same disease. Since they occur (usually) in order, let's look at them in the pattern people usually suffer them:

First signs of odontosis show up in children as cavities. Remember, now, that cavities are *symptoms*. Forget anything you may have been told, or assumed, that leads you to think of cavities as a disease, because they are not. They are symptoms of the initial form of odontosis, which Oramedics Fellows have named "Cariosis."

The term cariosis comes from your dentist's word for cavities, "caries;" "—osis" on the end of a word simply implies a disease process. (Incidentally, odontosis is a word derived from the Greek "odontos" —teeth —and the same —osis ending, meaning disease.)

The second stage of odontosis is normally gum irritation and minor infection. Dentists call the *symptoms* of this "gingivitis," from the Latin word for gums, "gingivae." The "itis" ending implies inflammation or infection. Oramedics Fellows know this disease as "gingivosis." Bear with this, because we're not simply playing word games, some kind of semantics shuffleboard. It's critical for your understanding of this whole subject, and ultimately your oral health, to understand that the "old" names and methods were all oriented toward symptoms. The Oramedics names relate to diseases, and it's these *diseases* we want to understand and destroy.

So we've introduced the family, "odontosis," and two of its members: "Cariosis" and "gingivosis." The third member of the family is the sneakiest, the deadliest; the one that will rob you of all your teeth and much of your health. This bad actor's name is "Periodontosis." Dentists actually agree that *this* is a disease, and they call it periodontal disease, or sometimes periodontitis. A more popular layman's term for it is pyorrhea.

We want you to think of the three members of the family as separate, because they occur in progression and have different symptoms; different effects on your oral and physical health. But we also want you to develop the understanding that while they are separate in nature, all three are actually caused by the same thing and all three, in reality, are extensions of the one disease now known as odontosis.

This disease begins with germs which are usually found in the human mouth sometime after birth. We don't have these at first, but they are introduced shortly afterward in a number of ways. For example: Mama wants to feed her baby some mush or baby oatmeal, but she's a loving mother: She wants to make sure it isn't too hot. What does she do? Naturally, she dips the spoon into the dish, daintily "samples" the mixture to make sure it's not too hot (or sweet, or cold, or bitter...) —and then she gives it to the baby. She also infects the child with the germs of odontosis.

These germs are strains of *Streptococcus mutans* and *Lactobacillus acidophilus.* There —you see? Part of the "mystery" is already gone: The truth about dental disease —odontosis —begins with the knowledge that we have identified the cause. It isn't an unknown fear: It's well-known microbes. You'll be hearing a lot more about Strep. mutans and Lacto. as you continue this book.

Most researchers agree that when these germs are

8

free-floating in the mouth, or disorganized, they have little effect on oral or physical health. In fact, you may recall reading somewhere that Lactobacillus germs might even have a beneficial role elsewhere in the body, such as in digestion.

Strep. mutans has no beneficial role (that science is aware of) but it is —when disorganized —a relatively harmless germ because the body is so well protected against its invasions.

The way these germs cause odontosis begins very subtly, almost insidiously. Some of them manage to come into close association where their waste products form a residue which the natural "washing" action of saliva doesn't remove. These waste products include materials called "dextrans," which are sticky and virtually transparent. This sticky substance adheres to teeth and forms a film called "plaque."

Those who brush their teeth with any frequency will not have this plaque *in evidence* when they look into a mirror: The teeth that are visible are pretty and clean. It's the plaque you *don't* see that causes problems. And this would be a good place to remind you that since the U.S. Health Department says 98 out of 100 Americans are suffering from odontosis, and that two percent of the public appears to be immune, the statistical implication is that *nobody* knows how to brush his teeth well enough to remove both the seen and the unseen plaque.

When plaque adheres to teeth it provides a natural home for colonies of Strep. mutans and Lacto. Now these germs are organized. The mouth is a perfect germ incubator: The temperature is a near-constant 98.6 degrees with permanent moisture and, from a germ's-eye view, a never-ending abundance of food.

Comfortably nestled in the plaque film, warm and moist and well-fed, the colonized bugs achieve explosive growth. As new germs appear by the hundreds of thousands, all of them become dextran-generators; they are all plaque-builders. The cycle becomes apparent: More germs, more tightly organized; larger colonies creating more plaque to harbor even more germs...

The insidious part of all this is that when the germs have developed a colony of metropolitan size —the New York City of "strep" and "lacto" bugs —we still can't even see it; don't really know it's there!

Plaque can be seen, particularly when a person has been lax in caring for his teeth over a period of time. When enough of the substance has built up on visible surfaces of the teeth, it appears as a whitish-yellow mat; a layer of "gunk" on the teeth. The tongue can feel plaque, in this amount, as a "furry" sensation.

Seen or unseen, when germs colonize and organize in plaque they achieve an *anerobic environment.* This state, shielded from oxygen and atmosphere, is the environment these bugs like best of all. Now they begin secreting more than dextrans: They generate acids.

When the germs' diet contains sugar, acid production increases. When you eat raw sugar, as in candy, the acid production increases instantly, enormously; and doesn't taper off for several hours. Of course, that's why dentists advise us to avoid sugar and, in these conditions, that is really good advice.

The point is: What are we doing under these conditions? A *disease process* is at work; germs are invading our health. Sugar doesn't create the condition, it simply makes it worse. Why eliminate sugar without eliminating the condition that makes sugar "bad for you?"

The acid produced by the germs is trapped between the surface of the teeth (enamel) and the layer of plaque film. Here the acid begins degrading the calcium-based tooth enamel, which gets weaker and weaker. This process is known as a carious lesion. In its early development it can't properly be called a cavity; but it will become a cavity when the outer enamel is broached and the softer "insides" of the

10

tooth are exposed to germs, acids and debris.

This whole process is "cariosis" —the disease which produces the symptoms called cavities. It is during the development of this state that the second stage has its beginning, also.

Gingivosis begins when the plaque film hardens at and slightly below the line where the gums meet the teeth. This hardening material is called calculus or tartar. It will eventually resemble the deposits at the bottom of an old teakettle; will get very hard and tenaciously attached to the teeth, and its surface will be sandpaper-rough.

This forms a natural "dam" which interferes with the natural washing action of saliva. Germs colonize beneath the gums; more plaque and acid are produced and the calculus continues to build up and harden in place.

The gum tissue is only one cell thick. It is an incredibly strong tissue for its thickness, and it has an extremely important job to do, about which more will be said later. No matter how strong this tissue may be, it is no match for the rough surface of the calculus and the physical action of chewing, brushing and so on.

Sooner or later the gum tissue gets "holes" in it and opens avenues for infection. The clean, wholesome pink color is replaced by a more reddish tone and the gums begin to bleed easily. Congratulations: You now have active cariosis *and* gingivosis at the same time!

And now you are a prime candidate for stage three: Periodontosis. The disorder beneath the gums grows steadily worse. Now "pockets" form between the gums and the teeth, reaching deeper and deeper toward the base of the tooth where it is set into the jawbone.

Tiny, delicate filaments called "connective tis-sues" anchor the teeth to the gums, very reminiscent of guy wires on telephone poles. These tissues are not able to withstand the combined assault of germs, physical abuse, acids and decaying debris. They are destroyed.

11

When enough of these tissues are destroyed, the gums sag away from the teeth; the teeth have no lateral support and become loose in their bone sockets. Often the bone itself will be attacked, resulting in bone infection. Obviously, all the teeth are ready to fall out, or be pulled out. It's denture time, now.

Even though most or all of this has been new to the reader, there has been an odd familiarity about it. That familiarity is easily explained: You've been reading the truth about a disease process which has been a mystery to you before; but you *did* know the symptoms.

It went something like this: "Kids get cavities" and maybe lose some of their teeth. Then, as people get older, they have trouble with tender, bleeding gums. As age sets in more and more, that trouble seems to get worse and worse until finally, they lose all of their teeth. And there is nothing anybody can do about this except, maybe, slow it down.

Now you know: The paragraph above may have seemed familiar, may even have seemed like "the truth" as everybody seems to understand it. Having learned that none of these things have to happen; that there is a disease with an identified cause, you can view dental disease from a new viewpoint.

It's nasty, sure. It's dangerous and painful and costly, we know. But it is *no longer* a total mystery; and it is going to become more and more understandable as you continue reading.

And, finally: All dental disease is totally preventible. Everybody understands about germs and their relationship to physical health. The disease we don't know is a terror; the disease we understand is defeated. That's the way it was with malaria, with polio, with diptheria, with hepatitis...with many once-frightening diseases which are now found mostly in history books.

Odontosis —cariosis, gingivosis and periodontosis —are now in the same category. We can win this war, too; you can win it personally. No less a reference than the Bible tells us "The truth will set you free..."

—Oramedics' motto is "freedom from dental disease."

Taken together, these two quotations set the theme for this entire book: The truth *will* set you free from dental disease.

Chapter Three
...that No Doctor is Going to Tell You

Isn't that an amazing statement? "The truth about dental disease...that no doctor is going to tell you..." Who would make such an assertion in our day and place; implying that medical and dental doctors are engaged in some huge, ugly conspiracy to defraud American patients?

Obviously one of two things can be assumed: Either the person who makes that statement is, plainly speaking, a nut-case fanatic...or there exists *circumstances* which prevent doctors from reaching the public with this information.

The latter is the case. Medical doctors don't tell us about these things because for nearly two centuries now, the mouth has been "out of bounds" for M.D.'s. It just isn't expected of medical doctors to provide training or counseling about "dental disease" any more than a dental doctor would be consulted for a broken ankle.

The American Medical Association would probably sanction any M.D. who began publicly and frankly discussing diseases of the mouth the teeth. We can't, in all fairness and honesty, imply that M.D.'s have abdicated their responsibility: Instead, we need only to realize that the development of health care delivery systems has circumstantially *relieved* M.D.'s of this responsibility.

Generations ago doctors were trained to care for the whole body; but there came a time when the dental profession split away from the medical profession. As the two went their separate ways, colleges began to specialize in dentistry and, ultimately, offer this as their exclusive "product."

Associations were formed; customs were established and as years passed, these customs became first "ethics" and, ultimately, laws. The net effect of this was to render oral health "off limits" to medical doctors and, today, no living "emdee" (MD) has ever thought of the mouth as part of "his" responsibility.

Is the M.D. at fault? —Of course not. Why on earth would we "blame" doctors for doing what they are clearly supposed to do? —Or, in the case of dental disease, we can hardly blame M.D.'s for *not doing* what they have traditionally, ethically and maybe legally been aware they are *not* supposed to do.

As it relates to medical doctors, then, if there is a conspiracy of silence it is equally a conspiracy of circumstance. Probably every M.D. in the country would understand the processes of dental disease and oral health if he gave it his professional attention. Doctors are trained and deeply experienced in microbiology, pathology and diagnosis/treatment methods. It is likely that a medical doctor would understand odontosis almost intuitively, if he looked into it.

Why should he?

As the popular young "Chico" of TV fame in the program, "Chico And The Man" would have said, "It's not my job..."

All right, then...whose "job" is it; to first develop a total understanding of dental disease and then, in turn, to inform the public? It's the "job" of the dental profession, obviously. Why haven't dentists done their job?

Traditionally, dentistry has been symptom-oriented. Many medical problems began this way, also. When science didn't have the answers to causes and cures of disease, doctors were forced to attend to symptoms. Throughout history, there have been maladies for which the only prognosis was to help the patient rest as comfortably as possible until he died... or recovered.

This is the unfortunate "state of the art" in dentistry, today. Because the profession either cannot or will not respond to dental disease in a medical, preventive approach, all that's left to the dentist is the task of helping the patient's mouth "rest comfortably" while the teeth "die."

Whole sub-sciences have become an integral part of the medical profession in the past decades. Such areas as microbiology and pathology, to name only a few, have wide application in research about the causes, effects and cures of diseases. Doctors almost universally are oriented toward correcting problems; toward curing and preventing disease, with less and less accent on trying to ease the symptoms.

For example: One of the good reasons doctors are so adamant about not mis-using antibiotics is that some disease symptoms are masked while the disease itself is not eliminated. In a typical situation, a person has a half bottle of oral penicillin lying about in the medicine cabinet from a recent illness (his or another family member's). When he feels out of sorts and decides he has "a bug," the person takes the antibiotic. Soon the symptoms recede...and the person smugly decides he's just saved himself another doctor's bill and the cost of a new prescription.

Wrong! Several days later we see this person at the emergency room of a hospital; or seated in a doctor's office, sweating and shaking like a leaf. The symptoms he covered up could have told the doctor, earlier, that this patient was headed for big trouble... could have told him early enough to head off that trouble.

So it is also with odontosis, with the various forms of dental disease. Dentists can address themselves to the symptoms (that's usually all they do); but the disease itself is there, masked and undercover, ready to break out with renewed strength.

As the patient leaves the dentist's office with a new filling in place and all the remaining teeth freshly cleaned and polished, he may think that he's done his best toward dental health. The sad truth is that even as he walks away from the dentist's office, odontosis is already regrouping its forces; already looking for a place to recolonize and continue its dirty work. As a matter of fact, the dentist may well have helped spread the disease to other parts of the mouth, areas which were uninfected before he began his examination. (More about this startling statement in a later chapter.)

The dentist is trained, and trained well, in reparative or restorative, mechanical dentistry. This means that he is concerned only with the technical aspects of a "symptom-fixing" approach to the teeth, themselves. He knows about the physical makeup of the mouth; he's been trained in anatomy and essential medicine. His days in dental school were filled with classes which are not unlike those attended by medical doctors. While the M.D. may have had more depth, and had other emphasis placed on what he learned; the D.D.S. has an amazing amount of training about overall human health.

It is the emphasis of his training that begins the process which the dentist follows for the remainder of his professional life. That emphasis is, of course, on teeth; to the exclusion or diminution of all else. The further "into dentistry" the doctor goes, the more he begins to exclusively concentrate on "fixing teeth" (or replacing them).

Thus there is one part of the human body that is "no man's land" to the medical and health sciences. That part, of course, is the mouth. Medical doctors and those involved in medical research all avoid the mouth because that is, as a matter of ethics and law, the domain of the dentist. Dentists, however, are almost exclusively concerned with only one part of the mouth: Teeth. This situation was summed up by Clinton T. Messner, D.D.S., chief of dental service for the U.S. Public Health Service:

"The medical profession has backed away from the oral cavity, leaving it as the province of the dentist, but the dentist has thought only of the welfare of the teeth. He has been so busy devising ways and means of replacing lost tooth structures that he has, in a measure, neglected the equally large field of the oral cavity itself."

Doctor Messner's comments continued, taking his profession to task, with this accurate but all-too-easily forgotten statement:

"Our dental magazines are filled with measures and methods whereby we might help to prevent disease of the teeth and gums, but little attention is given to the control of the spread of communicable diseases; and yet the field in which we work is the site of 90 percent of all infection which enters the body."

How important is a clean, healthy mouth...a disease-free oral ecology? To Doctor Messner, at any rate, the importance of a healthy mouth lies somewhere in the range of 90 percent of all human disease exposure. How important is this to dentists? "...He has been so busy devising ways and means of replacing lost tooth structures that he has, in a measure, neglected the equally large field of the oral cavity itself."

Doctor Messner indicates that dentists "in a large measure" ignore oral health. How large is that measure? Doctor Messner didn't choose to use language which would express the extent to which the dental profession has forsaken oral medicine; to what extent dentists are not interested in disease cure and prevention.

It may well be that this is a subjective evaluation at best —how would you back up an opinion which said two-thirds, or three-fourths, or any number of dentists were lax in their approach to oral health?

Let's approach it from another avenue. Instead of trying to express an opinion as to how prevalent this attitude may be, let's just look at a fact; a statistic, and see if that has any bearing on the attitude of today's conventional dentist. The fact: 98% of the people in the U.S. today are suffering from some form and degree of dental disease, according to the U.S. Public Health Service. The question: How many dentists are involved in cure or prevention of dental disease? The answer...?

An opinion will do; yours is invited at this point.

While there is no way to make a flat statement that advances in oral health have been retarded mostly because this one area of physical health is a "no man's land," it is at least good common sense to reach that conclusion. While truly significant research has seen progress in medical science, with one breakthrough after another, there is a strange silence from the dental world.

What research is being done? Tabloid "newspapers" describe with monotonous regularity a mysterious pill soon to reach the market that will immunize us all against dental disease. Someday, when astrologers are licensed to practise dental medicine, we will see these predictions come to pass...but for now, what is being done? Is anything being done? —And if it is; why are news media so reluctant to print it? *Why won't anybody tell us anything about dental disease?*

What doctor would tell you? Not the medical doctor: He's not involved in oral health. Certainly not the medical specialist-researcher: He's off on a fast track somewhere, studying the implications of disease and/or remedies elsewhere in the body or mind.

And don't expect to hear it from the dentist: What research *is* being done in dental/oral health is a crystal-clear *indictment* of the dental profession. If today's dentist wants to tell us the truth, the whole truth, and nothing but the truth, he must first learn it himself; then and only then could he tell us about it. Ah: But to do this, he would have to renounce his brothers and admit his own guilt. He would have to be willing to say, to anyone:

"The repair and replacement I've been making all my living doing for people was a stop-gap. I haven't been treating disease, I've been treating symptoms. I have no excuse other than that I thought that's what the people wanted...and because that's what my professional codes of ethics made me do..."

Who has the courage to do this, knowing that

instant reprisal will follow from the organization; knowing that it is most likely he will lose his license and be drummed out of the rolls of his societies? Before the reader judges dentists, as individuals, too harshly; let him stop for a moment and consider whether he himself could summon up that kind of courage.

Tough, isn't it? Until the American public and its government learn the truth and raise enough outcry, the institutions of organized dentistry will be able to control all dentists through fear. Even those who secretly want to stop doing "business as usual" are inhibited. If dentistry is ever to come of age, it will have to be from outside force. The only tether strong enough to pull such a reluctant jackass into the 20th century is the "rope" of public opinion and pressure.

That public pressure will only come after the people are informed about the sad, sorry state of affairs in America's oral health. That task, informing the public, should be a job for the profession...and for obvious reasons, the profession isn't going to do it.

The next thing we have to rely on is the public media: Newspapers, TV, radio and books. In another chapter we'll take a look at why the media has failed us in this case; again it's more a conspiracy of ignorance than any wilful intent to share that ignorance.

Until there is a groundswell of public sentiment, the task of telling America has to fall on those few who are aware of the state of things and are willing and able to tell others about it.

As of now, that includes you: As you learn more and more, either charity or obligation toward your fellow man should impel you to tell others. It might very well be that if you don't tell another person, that person will never know these things. If you don't tell him, who will? Without you, how will he learn the truth about the health of his mouth and body...

...that no doctor is going to tell him?

Chapter Four
The Inside Story: About the Mouth

What do you know about the inside of your mouth? What's in there? How does it work —or stop working? How much does it have to do with your overall health?

If you're like most of us, you'll shrug your shoulders and say something to the effect that there are teeth in the mouth, and a tongue. Pressed hard for information, you might add that the tongue has something to do with chewing as well as the sense of taste; that there are things in there (somewhere) called saliva glands that help you (inelegantly) make spit, and that the whole ensemble seems to work pretty well day in and day out without a lot of attention.

It hardly occurs to people to compare the mouth to, say, a laboratory incubator: But it should. The temperature is a mean average 98.6 degrees; the humidity is about 100%, the food sources for bacteria are almost endless in variety and abundance. Another good comparison might be to a housing authority —a condominium for germs —that is an equal opportunity landlord: There is room for all. For germs that thrive in the presence of oxygen, there's plenty of that; for those who prefer the absence of oxygen (anerobic) the mouth manages to accomodate these, also.

Let's take a "walk-through" the mouth; looking at it through the eyes of a person dedicated to understanding it as a unified system rather than an accidental site for a bunch of things called teeth that provide dentists with an income. Only by understanding how all of the parts of the mouth interact with environment do we begin to get some insight about odontosis —dental disease —and its prevention.

In the preceding chapter it became evident that medical doctors are not ordinarily interested in anything having to do with the oral cavity (mouth); having more or less deeded that territory over to dentists. It was also pointed out that dentists concentrate totally upon the teeth, now and then becoming concerned (far, far too late) about the condition of the gums.

Who cares about the rest of the mouth? The answer is simple —and simply ridiculous: Nobody cares; and that usually includes the person who more than anyone *should* care...the person whose life and health depends upon it.

The mouth begins with the lips, which medical students quickly learn to call the "vermillion border." If they manage to learn this terminology well enough to "hang onto it" until they pass that exam, they probably soon stop thinking in terms of borders. After all, lips are lips; doctors are not often concerned with them and dentists almost never.

Why do they call lips a "border?" —Because at this point of your anatomy one of the most important structural changes takes place. The lips are truly the border between the "outside" and the "inside" of the body. The lips begin on the outside, where there is facial skin. This skin is made up of cells called epithelium, layer upon layer. It isn't uncommon for external skin to be made up of hundreds of layers of this cellular material, in areas such as the feet, etc., where nature expects "wear and tear" on the body.

Tender, delicate skin areas have fewer layers of epithelium. This is why it's easier to cut yourself, or get scratched or burned more easily and painfully, in areas of fewer cell layers.

That's what the lips are all about. They begin with facial "skin" several layers thick and, as we move into the mouth, there are fewer and fewer layers of cells.

On the inside, as the lips gradually become the interior walls of the mouth, this cellular layer ultimately diminishes to the thickness of one cell. How thick is skin that's "one cell thick?" Measurements dealing with things this tiny lose all meaning. Instead, let's use an illustration:

If you took the "skin" from an area inside the

mouth —a piece about the size of a postage stamp, for instance —and then cured it so that it was perfectly flat and stiff, you could look at it with no trouble. Then, if you took that "postage stamp" and held it so you were looking at the edge instead of the front or back...it would disappear. One thickness of epithelium is too small to be seen with the human eye.

Epithelium has a most amazing property; it is this property that nature programmed into it to keep us safe from disease and infection. Without it, without this unique ability epithelium has coded into its genetic material, we'd all be dead in a very short time.

That magic capability is that epithelium is a germ barrier; as well as being a barrier to an endless array of poisons, chemicals and other "things" which would be harmful to us. As an example, you could take a culture of virulent hepatitis germs and rub it on your forearm: If there was no scratch, no break in the epithelium, there would be no disease. Wash it off with germicide and relax. However —if any of those germs found the tiniest scratch, abrasion or break in the epithelium... wham! You've had it!

That's one of the major roles of the tissue lining inside the lips, the mouth, on the surface of the gums ...throughout the oral cavity: There is barrier surface which protects you from infection. When you recall that the interior of the mouth is a nature-perfect incubator for almost any kind of germ that manages to find its way past the lips, the importance of this un-broken barrier wall is understood.

Another unsung hero of the oral cavity is the saliva gland. These little fountains produce the solution we call saliva, 24 hours a day. Without it, the mouth would dry out; skin would crack, elasticity would be lost. It is easy to realize the importance of saliva in keeping the mouth lubricated, in helping to mix with food as you chew to produce the required consistancy for digestion.

What has not been generally understood about saliva is the function it plays in the health of the teeth.

23

One important task is to keep the mouth washed. The constant bathing action helps move food particles, debris, and unwanted germs through the mouth into the alimentary canal —the digestive system —and eventually through the body. When there's some problem that's too hard to handle with this constant, gentle "current" passing through the system, our reflexes tell us to do something about it:

We spit the problem out. Sip something by accident that's too bitter, or too hot; or which we realize a split-second too late is dangerous, and immediately we react: Out it goes! How does this happen? The moment we need to repel the invader, whatever it may be, the saliva glands go into emergency production. The resulting flood of saliva helps expel the foreign matter.

This is why you suffer the indignity and discomfort of over-active saliva glands when you're strapped into the dentist's chair: When fingers, instruments and debris are introduced into the mouth, the saliva glands do their thing. It is these little guys that have helped Oramedics coin a rather inelegant term for conventional dentistry: "Drill, spit and fill."

Saliva has another role in the health of the teeth; one which has only recently received any attention in research laboratories; one which many dentists may not be aware of.

Although the amount of research being conducted with respect to oral microbiology, pathology, and ecology is almost criminally nil, there is some ongoing research: It has recently demonstrated absolutely that early cavities, one of the first symptoms of odontosis, can heal themselves if infection-causing germs are eliminated. How does this happen?

The saliva helps coat the initial damage, the early carious lesion of tooth enamel, with a chemical solution. This is a complex formula: For our purposes, we need only consider that at least part of the formula has to do with deposits of calcium, the building-blocks of bone structure.

The essential discovery is this: In the absence of disease-producing pathology (germs), normal and healthy saliva plays a significant...if not major...role in the process of reversing cavity damage. Teeth can heal themselves; and saliva is one of the unsung heros of this heretofore unsuspected truth.

The next part of the mouth that needs to be considered is the gums. It is here that most of the damage to oral health occurs; it is here that the most advanced odontosis does its dirty work. Gum problems —not teeth problems —are responsible for loss of teeth in adults. And nobody really knows what enormous percentage of all human physical disease, disorder and malfunction has its onset through a breakdown of gum tissue.

Simply stated, the business of the gums is to hold the teeth in place, upright in their sockets in the jawbone. This is accomplished by microscopic filaments which anchor the tooth to the gum tissue, providing support without being inflexible. Perhaps a good analog is to think of guy wires on telephone poles: The "connective tissue" of the guy wire holds the pole upright without, itself, being rigid. Of course you'd picture the telephone pole with two or three such guy wires at most; and the connective tissues between teeth and gums are so numerous as to be almost dense...but that's the picture.

Because of this ingenious natural design, the teeth can exert pressures of up to 30,000 pounds per square inch while biting and chewing foods, without being displaced in the bone socket. These pressures come from an infinite variety of axes...from every direction... as the teeth grind away. The support must hold steady from all forces, vertical and lateral, and it does. And yet, it must remain flexible at these enormous pressures: If there was no provision for "shock absorbers" we'd break enamel and bone; we'd tear tissues and ligaments.

It's easy to see why these connective tissues are

the most important element of keeping firm, healthy teeth in their appointed places. Without them, you could grasp a tooth in your fingertips and wrench it from its socket. We're fortunate that these tissues were designed by God and Mother Nature to last for a natural lifetime.

Of all the tissues in the mouth, these are the ones we must be most concerned with protecting. Indeed, without these tissues, there could be no teeth as we know them. Most dentists will tell you that once these connective tissues are gone (destroyed), they are never replaced. Oramedics doesn't necessarily agree with that —that they cannot be replaced naturally —but we are not aware of any independent research that would show what happens to connective tissues *in the absence* of disease.

Dentists have not observed restoration or replacement of connective tissue; research has not documented it —but couldn't that be because they are still using the frame of reference that dental disease is *natural* to the environment?

Almost everyone knows somebody who has had teeth "knocked loose" through some accident. Didn't the teeth eventually "tighten up" again? Why was that? —Wasn't it because the connective tissue that was torn or stretched *grew back*? There is usually no disease that far down on the tooth structure; at least not until the terminal phase of periodontosis. Ask yourself why, in an environment free from disease, those teeth were able to "tighten up"...unless the connective tissues somehow "got healed."

Accidents that harm connective tissue are relatively rare. Ordinarily, instinct and the natural protection inside the mouth makes such accidents fortunately few and far between.

What usually happens to connective tissue is a disease: The disease is one we call periodontosis, a member of the odontosis family; and your dentist probably calls it periodontal disease. A more common

26

name for it is pyorrhea.

We'll talk about this disease in more detail later. For now, you should understand that the connective tissue you just met...and discovered to be one of your best friends in this lifetime...has only one natural enemy. That enemy, odontosis, will destroy connective tissue and when that happens, you will lose all of your teeth. Not a pleasant picture, is it?

As you learn more and more about oral health and medicine, you will understand that most of the damage done by odontosis is either reversible —it can heal itself —or repairable, in that teeth can be mechanically restored when they're too far gone for natural healing.

Dentistry today is so far behind research that most dentists aren't aware of the natural healing processes which can occur in a disease-free environment. There is, today, no definitive research which proves that connective tissue can restore itself; and nothing that mankind has yet devised as a substitute can take its place.

So we can't prove that these tissues heal; and we can't offer any hope of artificial "help." If you're a typical American adult, you've already lost connective tissue to disease. There is still enough (if you still have most of your teeth) to keep them in place and healthy, but some of it is gone and more of it is threatened with every day that passes while odontosis is active in your mouth.

There should be no question but that, since odontosis is preventible, you'd want to prevent it. There's no reason to suffer from a disease we know how to cure. It should become even more important when you realize that day by day you are losing the one most important tissue able to prevent tooth loss.

Perhaps the most-understood part of your mouth —its teeth —requires the least explanation. Because dentistry has had such a single-purpose preoccupation with teeth since it became a separate branch of medicine, there has been a continuing attempt by some dental writers to acquaint the public with its teeth.

Most people know that teeth are covered with an outer layer of enamel; the stuff that gives them nicknames such as "pearly whites." Many know that underneath the enamel is a substance called dentin which is essentially the same as enamel but much softer and more vulnerable; and that the next strata is called "pulp," which term pretty well explains what it is. In the "roots" of the tooth are nerve chambers and the tissues that keep the tooth "alive" through nourishment, etc.

We are ordinarily only concerned with the enamel, because that's the part of the tooth that we brush (or forget to brush); because that's the part of the tooth that we present to our neighbors every day as a fairly accurate symbol of how highly we regard our own appearance and health. The enamel is where we "get cavities."

What we don't often think about is that enamel, like epithelium (skin) tissue, is a germ barrier also. You can bathe clean, healthy tooth enamel with disease germs and they'll simply wash off.

Not so with the next layers down. Once the enamel is pierced —by anything, but usually by a cavity —there is an "open sesame" for germs to get into a part of the body that has no defense against infection. Perhaps the fastest way to get this point across is to use shock technique: You could get syphilis through a cavity faster than through ordinary sex. And *that's* a fact!

A paragraph or so ago, we noted that "clean, healthy tooth enamel" had the barrier property of simply rejecting germs. Let's take another look at that, because there were two words there that are too important to miss. If the teeth are *not* clean, they must have an invisible film of plaque on them; and if they do, they can't avoid the germs. True: The enamel barrier is still operating, the germs infesting the film of dirty plaque are effectively separated from the vulnerable part of the tooth. However, those germs will colonize in that plaque and create by-products; and those by-products will contain chemicals. Those chemicals will attack the enamel and ultimately cause a cavity. When that happens, the tooth is no longer healthy (or clean): Disease in some form, perhaps in many forms, is the inevitable result.

One other bit of information about teeth is helpful; having to do with the way teeth are shaped and how closely-placed they may be. The design of the "big" teeth in your mouth, the bicuspids and molars, your "chewing teeth," is different from the "biters" at the front of your mouth. Put the tip of your tongue on your "eye teeth," the canines or incisors, three or four back from the top front teeth. If yours are "normal" (and they are), those teeth are quite pointed and sharp. The ones in front of those have edges more or less like chisels: They're wide, relatively thin front-to-back, and have cutting edges.

Now run your tongue over your "chewers" on the top and bottom. Notice that these teeth are fatter, some of them almost round or oval shaped, and that the chewing surfaces are flat; even dished in. A bit more exploring with the tongue tells you that this dished-in portion is not smooth, like the inside of a bowl or saucer, but has little hills and valleys. (Dentists call these pits and fissures).

The next thing you can learn with your tongue, or a toothpick, is that the space between teeth is always narrow. In fact, you may not be able to insert a flat toothpick between some adjacent teeth: To all intents and purposes, there just isn't any space between them.

All of these things in the shape and location of the teeth are vitally important to nature because it is the shape and location of the teeth that allows us to bite, to chew, to do all of the things good health and good nourishment demands of our teeth.

They are vitally important to us, trying to learn how to defeat odontosis, because these shapes and locations are often hard to clean properly. It is in these hidden-from-view areas that we are prone to "miss" with our brush, or ignore with floss or dental tape, that odontosis has its field day.

That space between two teeth that you think of as touching each other is, from a germ's viewpoint, large enough to establish New York City. Once plaque settles between adjacent teeth, you may be sure that germs will find it. Leave them alone for long enough, and you will have a cavity there. Ignore that cavity if you will; and the next thing that happens is gum tissue "problems" that become gum tissue disease.

As a matter of fact, even if we brush and floss or tape properly —something that only perhaps two percent of America's people even know how to do —there's no guarantee that we'll eliminate all of the colony-producing plaque in these pit and fissure areas or between adjacent teeth.

Sometimes the only absolutely certain way to prevent bacterial infestation is through medicine: A mouthrinse that contains the chemicals which spell sudden death to odontosis germs. There'll be more about this rinse technique when we get to the part dealing with oral medicine.

Now that you understand the inside of your mouth a little better, think for a moment about the amazing fact that no dentist ever mentioned this to you. There is no way to consider teeth and their health as separate from gums and connective tissue. To think of the state of our dental health as totally unrelated to the lining of the mouth, or as separate from the function of saliva, is incredible. And yet, we Americans are subjected for our entire lifetime with a branch of medical science that would totally ignore everything except teeth, as if they were not connected to the rest of the body.

The amazing thing is not that our mouths can be...and are...the source of a major portion of all physical ills and diseases: What's truly amazing is that we're not all dead before our 21st birthday! When

30

you consider that individuals —and medical/dental science —have simply ignored this whole area of physical health, then you begin to have some appreciation of how incredibly tough and resilient the mouth really is.

If our mouth and its elements; tissues and teeth and bone and saliva-producers and all of these other carefully-orchestrated things can take such good care of us when we ignore them...

Think of how healthy they would be if *we* took care of *them,* instead of the other way around.

Chapter Five
Germ Warfare

Most people today still believe in the old "truths" about dental disease; truths which are really myths and have been for many decades. Your own frame of reference is undergoing change as you discover, for yourself, some of the modern developments that underscore the insights of yesterday's unsung heros of dentistry.

Doctors Levi Parmly and G.V. Black were two such dentists who stood head and shoulders above the rest of the profession in past generations. These men gave the profession insight and some goals to aim for: The profession ignored them; the general public, by and large, never heard of them.

Today there is a group of dentists confederated under the banner of Oramedics International who are trying to bring this modern information out of the dental profession and into the hands of all people. The most significant reason these men want to deliver this is not to help people become dentists...but to force dentists to become people who help.

If the profession will not use modern science and technology left to its own devices, the public is the only "agency" which can bring pressure to bear. The state laws are written by the dental associations; the dental associations consider themselves to *be* the law and practicing dentists consider themselves accountable only to their professional societies.

This brief philosophical statement was necessary, as an introduction to this chapter, because we are going to get into some fairly detailed and technical information. The reader may find himself asking, "Why do I have to know all this stuff?"

We wanted to remind you of this book's subtitle: "What you need to know about the health of your mouth and body —that no doctor is going to tell you." It is not enough that you know some highlights about the process of dental disease —odontosis —because if we give you only the surface information, you will have no ammunition to use in future conversations with dentists when you want adequate oral medical attention.

It isn't enough to change your frame of reference. We have to give you detailed information so that, when your own oral health is at stake, you can change the *dentist's* frame of reference. In short, you'll have to be able to convince the dentist that you simply will not settle for "drill, spit and fill" dentistry any more...and the only way you'll be able to do that is to jolt him out of his complacency by your knowledge.

He will want to repair symptoms.

You will want to discuss disease.

He will want to talk about techniques, amalgams, instruments, false teeth and extractions.

You will have to make him learn a whole new method of approaching dental disease: Instead of fighting a losing, symptom-fixing battle, he is going to have to learn a different kind of "fighting:"

Germ Warfare.

Earlier in this book we briefly looked at the mechanics of odontosis. Let's recap, now, the three stages of this disease's progress:

Cariosis is the initial stage of odontosis. It derives its name from the word "caries," which your dentist understands as his word for cavities. The cavity, or carious lesion, is the major symptom of cariosis. While the cavity itself is not the disease, it is an effect which we instantly recognize; and so this stage of disease is named for its significant symptom.

The next stage is gingivosis. Again, this disease is named for its most prominent effect or symptom: An "osis" of the "gingivae," a disorder or infection of the gums.

The final stage of odontosis is periodontosis: This arch criminal is also known as periodontal disease or pyorrhea.

These three stages may overlap —they often do —and they may not occur in sequence, in every case. In the majority of cases, however, they will occur in this order, one blending into the other. In early years we will "get cavities," meaning that we are suffering from cariosis; the next problem will be sore, tender and easily-bleeding gums, a sure sign that we've graduated to gingivosis; and, finally, the infection, loose teeth and general depreciation of fitness and health tells us we are now in stage three: Periodontosis.

The entire spectrum of odontosis begins in an unseen invasion of bacteria. At birth we are free from the germs of odontosis but we never seem to remain exempt for long. Quite often, babies are "inoculated" with the germs which will ultimately destroy their teeth...by their own mothers.

No loving mother would do anything to harm her own baby, so to make sure the food she is about to feed the infant is at the right temperature, consistency and taste, she samples it.

If it seems okay to mother, the remaining food on the spoon is promptly inserted into baby's mouth ...along with the first invasion of germs.

This same mother wouldn't dream of sampling baby's food if she were suffering from a disease she understands —such as a common cold, or any of the infectious diseases we are all familiar with. She knows better than to transfer disease germs to a helpless infant.

But —before now —who ever told mama that she could transmit *bad teeth germs*? Isn't it amazing, when you stop to think about it, that everyone simply accepts as a fact that bad teeth "just happen" —that there is no *cause* for this disease? Before you read this far in this book, would you have ever dreamed of connecting the adult's bad teeth with future dental disease in an infant that, today, doesn't even *have* any teeth?

This, of course, is just one of the ways in which the germs enter the mouth to set up their germ warfare. By the time the first teeth show through an infant's gums, there is already the beginnings of odontosis present: The person has *Streptococcus mutans* and *Lactobacillus acidophilus* germs in his mouth.

Is this invariably and inevitably the case? For all practical purposes, yes it is. The U.S. Government publishes data that says perhaps two percent of the population appear to have a natural immunity to odontosis. Until Oramedics International began compiling and concentrating on late research, nobody ever had any idea of why there was a natural immunity. The secret of this immunity is still locked away in nature, but research into the activity of certain enzymes shows promise for the future.

For today —and the forseeable future —we need only realize that 98 out of 100 people will have the Strep. mutans and Lacto. germs present in their oral ecology; if not before they actually have any teeth, then certainly not long afterward.

These germs have never been associated with any particularly dangerous activity in the human body other than their assault on oral health. Neither Strep. mutans or Lacto. are implicated in any other disease process so far known to medical science. Lactobacillus, in fact, has been considered beneficial elsewhere in the gastro-intestinal tract: Some health researchers believe it would be harmful to eliminate this microbe entirely from the system. In the mouth, however, Lacto. is Public Enemy No. 2 —following immediately behind Strep. mutans as the Bad Bug of oral health.

It would be ideal for our dental health if we could totally and forever eliminate these germs from the oral ecology; but that is impractical —we'd simply become re-inoculated as time went by —and it isn't really all that necessary.

When these germs are in a free-floating state, when they are just present in the mouth in a disorganized fashion, there is no evidence that suggests they are harmful or dangerous. The incidence of these germs will be below certain levels if the person "checks out" in a saliva culture; the reduced numbers of these germs will indicate that they have not formed organized colonies.

It is when these guys begin settling down, raising families and building Germ City, USA inside your mouth that the trouble begins. And it begins in a way that you can neither see nor feel: Some of the Strep. mutans germs will adhere to an invisible film on the surface of the teeth, stake their claim, and begin reproducing.

These germs ingest their food from debris, food particles and sugars in your mouth; and they secrete their own waste products. One of these wastes is called dextran. It is an invisible product that "plates out" on the tooth surface, leaving a film called plaque. Interestingly enough, the word "plaque" is from the French language, "plaquer," and it translates, roughly, "to plate" or coat —a very aptly named substance.

You can't see plaque unless you ignore it until it has built up many, many layers thick. Then it will be visible as an off-white or yellowish "mat" on the teeth.

Often, you'll feel plaque with your tongue before you ever see it in the mirror. It is the fuzzy feeling, the "something wrong" feeling on your teeth; the "yuck" of the early-morning trip to the bathroom. Another sure sign of the germ activity and plaque buildup is something our society has turned into a "capital offense" in society: You'll have bad breath.

Many people who are faithful tooth-brushers will not have plaque in evidence, either by feel or by visual inspection in the mirror. They will be able to pass the "social exam" of getting close to someone else without destroying the relationship. Such people may believe they've eliminated plaque...and they have, in all the places where it is relatively harmless.

Don't misunderstand —plaque is *never* harmless, no matter where it is found in the mouth. Where there's plaque, there's activity in the germ colonies; and where this activity exists, there's danger of odontosis.

It is just that the plaque which you can readily see and feel is on the broad, flat surfaces of your teeth where odontosis activity is least prevalent. Why? Well ...if you were to take a bite out of a firm apple, the colonies which had attempted to organize on your top front teeth would be wiped out.

True, these germs would simply re-organize and start over...but they'd have been temporarily "bushwhacked" in their business of destroying your health.

The places where you can't reach with your tongue or mirror...the areas between adjacent teeth, the pits and fissures of the molars...these are the plaque-laden areas which are shielded from natural chewing and saliva-washing action.

Thus, even though your teeth may be cosmetically clean, and your breath "refreshed," you will still be victimized by bacterial colonies.

The growth of these germs, once they begin the cycle of excreting dextrans to form plaque; then lodging in the plaque to reproduce and colonize, only to increase their dextran production, is nothing less than explosive. Now, if there are active Strep. and Lacto. colonies in your mouth, the count in a Lactobacillus saliva test might shoot up into the hundreds of thousands per milliliter.

When the plaque has built up enough that the germ colonies are shielded between the plaque and the surface of the tooth, they are no longer in an "aerobic" or oxygen based environment. This thickness of plaque might still not be enough for you to see or feel: To a germ, "thick" is so small as to be negligable. When the germs are in this oxygen-free, anerobic environment, they secrete acids among their waste products. These of course are the chemicals that, dammed against the tooth enamel by the protecting layer of plaque, begin to eat away at the surface of the tooth.

37

The acid de-calcifies the enamel, creating a carious lesion. Penetrating deeper and deeper, it finally pierces the barrier protection of the enamel and reaches the dentin beneath.

Remember, now...this dentin has no natural protection from germs; nor is it designed to exist in contact with the environment, any more than the meat or bone of your arm is expected to survive without its protecting layer of skin. The dentin begins to decay; it is subject to infection. The speed with which the cavity now progresses is considerably increased.

If the disease process had been halted early in this stage: If the germ colony was disorganized and most of the germs destroyed; and the plaque film done away with, the natural capability of healthy saliva would have gone to work in restoring the surface enamel of the tooth.

If the disease process *is not* halted, the cavity continues to bore its way deeper and deeper into the tooth, through the dentin and pulp and into the nerve chamber. As this process continues, germs from the mouth are given an ever-increasing access to the rest of the body through the circulatory system. Many of us are well aware of one of the effects of nerve-chamber infection: The disastrous swelling, pain and poison we call an abscess.

If that was the end of this horror story, it would be bad enough. Unfortunately for adult oral health, the cavity is just the beginning of sorrows. There's more: And the "more" that's coming will ultimately destroy all of your teeth; but not before it has done immeasurable damage to your overall health, not before it has cost you perhaps hundreds of dollars in dental and medical bills.

We Americans need to be jolted —hard —out of our misbelief that cavities are the key dental health problem. It's partly the "fault" of massive TV advertising for tooth-cleaning preparations; it's partly the fault of tradition...but it's mostly the fault of the dental profession: We Americans simply don't understand that cavities are the least of our problems with the mouth.

Odontosis will continue to wreak havoc with our health, but it will be through attacks on the gum tissue and connective tissue that holds our teeth in place. As we grow out of our teens we are less susceptible to cavities, but much more prone to have gingivosis and periodontosis. Given the mental attitude —the frame of reference —most of us are saddled with, we tend to view this lessening of cavities as evidence that our problems are "going away." They're just beginning.

Why doesn't the dental profession launch an all-out effort to educate the public about the realities of these secondary diseases? Why is it still apparently true that "no doctor is going to tell you these things?"

We can only make assumptions based on observed attitudes within the profession and its societies. It seems that dentists and their societies suffer from inertia: They are just as bound up in tradition and hampered by an obsolete frame of reference as the people they should be educating. To put it bluntly and not too politely: They may not know any better.

Another view is that the profession and its allied industries, the people who manufacture false teeth and lotions and potions and preparations and amalgams and all the trappings and tinctures and machinery connected with repairing and replacing teeth...just maybe these people don't want us to know how to prevent oral disease.

If we do, they're out of business.

Whatever the reasons behind the veil of silence on this subject, it's vital to your own personal health that you never again think of cavities as the number one enemy of your health. Obviously, we want to do away with cavities; obviously, you owe it to your children to help them have disease-free, healthy and pleasant teeth. Of course it's important to destroy the disease process at this first stage: Cariosis. That's what

Oramedics always tries to do. But the important thing to your adult health is to realize that the second and third stages of the disease are the ones *you* will suffer most from.

Gingivosis and ultimately periodontosis have their beginnings in the same plaque that is necessary for the germs to produce cavities. Plaque has long been implicated in the formation of deposits on and between the teeth, near the gumline, called tartar and/or calculus. These deposits are hard, resembling in both texture and color the mineral deposits often found inside old teakettles.

The tartar acts as a dam, impeding the normal flow of saliva; it helps trap food particles and it creates an excellent environment for germ colonizaton. Of course as germs are attracted to and by this condition, the dextran production is increased; therefore the plaque build-up increases, thereby accelerating further deposits of tartar and calculus...

And in the small area between the tooth and the gum; the place where the gum is not fastened to the tooth, the ecology becomes perfect for breeding germs. Now we are no longer talking about Strep. mutans and Lacto. alone: Now we have provided a warm, moist, food-filled haven where a long list of disease germs can set up shop and either form colonies or lie in wait for "something to happen" which will give them access through the barrier tissue into the unprotected tissue and circulatory system of the body.

The "something" happens fairly soon under these conditions. Because the surface of the deposits is very rough —it compares, for our purposes, with sandpaper —just think what it can do to a barrier tissue only one cell thick! Remember earlier when we described the "thickness" of the gum tissue? If you could look at it end-on, it would be too thin to see without a microscope.

Now, we are going to put that in contact with something very like sandpaper...and then we are going to apply up to 30,000 pounds per square inch pressure as we chew: Pressures which come from various angles, sometimes thrusting, sometimes grinding with a rotary motion.

There! And there! —We've abraided the tissue so much that the outer cell is penetrated. Germs rush to the spot; the walls are down, the gates are open...

Congratulations. You have gingivosis.

If you are like so many of us, you'll learn to live with it (at least, you don't seem to have so many tooth-aches as you did years ago, when you had all those cavities, right?). You can put up with the puffiness, the tenderness, the bleeding when you now and then brush your teeth "too hard." When you bite into an apple and are momentarily shocked to see the pink stain in the toothmarks —you manage to forget it within a few minutes. A good, expressive shrug of the should-ers helps with this because, after all, "doesn't every-body have the same problem? There isn't anything you can do about it, is there?"

Periodontosis is insidious. Look the word up in a dictionary, if you want to. Sneaky. It creeps up on you. You're "just about" like you were yesterday; maybe a bit worse than a month or so ago —but who really remembers how "bad off" you were a month or so ago?

Now and then you might feel a bulge partway down the outside of the gum; there may be a soreness there you didn't notice before. You might even think to your-self that there's a little pouch or pocket between your tooth and the gum. That's funny (odd) —you never noticed that before, did you?

You are right about one thing: There is a pocket there. Any dentist would tell you that; because that's what they call this phenomenon: Periodontal pockets.

They are cesspools. They are filled with debris from food, from the excrement of germs, from the fluid produced by your body's losing battle with germs (sorry about that, but the word is "pus"). Your breath smells like the inside of a sewerline and, unless you are very fortunate, your general health is declining. You quickly adapt by learning which foods, especially raw vegetables and others which are tough or rough —and very good for you —that you now have to avoid; or pay the price of pain and bleeding.

What do you suppose is happening down inside those pockets —other than that the barrier tissues have been long-since destroyed, and you are being attacked by germs and suffering from infection?

Do you remember the connective tissues we talked about earlier? Those are the "miniature marvels" that hold the tooth in place, anchored like guywires to the gums. One of the most significant points we noted was that these connective tissues can't be restored or replaced in a diseased environment. It is periodontosis which will destroy the tissues, as the disease progresses ever deeper, forming a larger pocket. The debris, the tartar and calculus, the germs and the chemicals are all "doing the number" on connective tissues, day in and day out.

The tissues are attacked directly by infections, abraided by debris and deposits, insulted by acids; they are stressed by the normal pressures of chewing, but under abnormal conditions. One by one, they are severed or fatigued or destroyed...and seldom if ever replaced.

The tooth gets looser and looser in its socket. As the disease pocket reaches the base of the tooth with its cargo of disorders, it begins to include the jawbone itself in its path. From this, you could end up with bone infection possibly requiring surgery. Even if that doesn't happen, however, you may rest assured that the prophecy that is, today, American common knowledge, will finally come true: You'll lose all your teeth.

But the corollary that goes along with that prophecy is obscene, knowing what you know now. The prediction is that we are going to lose all our teeth anyway; the corollary is that "there's nothing anyone can do about it."

There is most definitely something that can be done about it, and *you* can do it: This disease can be stopped in its tracks *at any point* in its progress. If that's done early enough, many of its damages can and will heal themselves. If it comes later, much of the damage can't heal —but it can usually be repaired. Only in its closing stages does some of the damage become medically or technically irreversable.

There's no need to feel that "it's too late now, anyway" —because when the disease process stops, the ongoing damage stops. Sure, there may be some repair needed...but *it isn't going to get any worse* if you do away with the cause. For whatever reason —financial, time, emotion —whatever keeps you from having the damage repaired, you can wait knowing that the worst is behind you.

This chapter has been a horror story, but even while you read the unvarnished truth about what causes odontosis, you were learning —probably for the first time —that this is a disease process with identifiable cause, predictable progress, and ultimate consequence. Almost every disease conquered by medical science has gone through this phase before it was overcome. First, we fear the unknown...then we name it, and understand it...and finally we learn how to cure it, or prevent it, or both.

That's the way it is with odontosis. We understand it, now, and we've come up with a cure and a prevention that's infallible when people apply these methods.

We personally think that the dental profession's failure to bring all these things together, and to tell the world about it, is an abdication of their responsibility of awesome magnitude.

If this was a "medical" disease, like polio or dyptheria or cancer, the medical profession would be helping to bring this knowledge to the people. Can you imagine, for example, that the profession would have tried to muzzle Dr. Jonas Salk; would have tried to prevent him from bringing the Salk Vaccine into the world to wipe out polio?

You must remember, however, that we are dealing now with a profession whose entire income...their very reason for existing...depends upon one disease, and only one.

When we get rid of dental disease, what happens to dentists?

If you're beginning to understand why you've never read before about the disease itself; think how much less likely you'd be to read about its cure. More than ever, what you'll begin learning in the next chapter helped us subtitle this book: "...that no doctor is going to tell you."

If you're taking exceptionally good care of your teeth, following religiously the programs you read about in the media; paying close attention to the TV commercials for various toothpastes, and doing more or less what your dentist tells you to do, there are two things you should know:

1. You are so unusual a person you should be pleased to learn that your efforts are rare indeed; and

2. Aside from social cosmetics (pleasant breath with a shining smile), you aren't doing your health much good at all.

We of course don't suggest that you quit keeping your teeth as clean as possible: There's no such thing as "too clean" when it comes to oral health. What we want you to understand...clearly...is that today's concepts of oral hygiene are simply inadequate and full of error.

Today's oral hygiene is sickening...and that's a fact. Let's take a close look at the most-publicized "regimen" that is supposed to promise dental health:

"Brush after meals, use floss, avoid sweets, and see your dentist twice a year." Do you do this? —Few people do. Why? Taken more or less in order: It is inconvenient to brush the teeth after every meal. After breakfast, there's the rush to get to school or to the office. After lunch...what are you supposed to do, sit at the counter in Pete's Diner and swab out your mouth? (Where do you spit...?) After supper, of course, there's the mad scramble for the living room to dispute over which TV channel should get preference: News Vs. the Wednesday Night Movies...

Use floss? (What's that?) —Many patients answer questions about dental floss, and the answers usually come out something like this: "It's hard to use..." "I don't have time..." "It hurts my fingers..."

"I try to use it, but it cuts my gums and they bleed..."

How many of us avoid sweets? In the U.S. today, our national diet is a cause of deep concern for nutritionalists. The growing movement toward health foods and real attention to nutritional values stems from an increasing awareness that our national diet is woefully unhealthy.

Ask any informed health-oriented person, such as those who are members of the National Health Federation: They'll tell you that one of the principal elements of their program to cleanse and rejuvenate the whole body *must* begin with a critical look at what they eat. Our intake of soft foods, loaded with highly-refined sugar, is highest in the "free" world. Among the "advanced" civilizations, the Americans are killing themselves with diet indulgence at an amazing rate.

What does this do to our oral health, not to mention our overall health? For our present purposes, let's just stick to the one comment: "Avoid sweets."

With today's diet, there is *no way* you are going to fulfill this requirement. You may avoid *some* sweets —the ones you incorrectly think you should avoid, such as chewing gum and candy, confections and delightful concoctions. We'll show you, later in this chapter, that the sweets you *do* avoid are less dangerous than the "sweets" you *don't* avoid...because nobody ever told you the difference. Want an example? You'd be better off chewing on a caramel candy than eating a slice of white bread, as far as your dental health is concerned! (More on this subject follows in a few pages.)

Finally: Do you see your dentist every six months? We are so brainwashed by commercials and "common knowledge" that many of us are ashamed to admit we don't make the twice-annual pilgrimage to the dentist. Some people do; with a religious determination that is commendable. Well, as the saying goes, we have some good news...and some bad news.

The good news is for those who can't seem to get to the dentist twice a year: It wouldn't make any difference, probably, if you did.

The bad news is for those who have written that twice-annual check for themselves and their children: Your trip to the dentist wasn't (probably) necessary and in many cases, you'd have been far better off if you'd stayed away...the dentist may have created more disease than he "fixed."

Now let's take another look at the formula: Brush after meals, use floss, avoid sweets, and see your dentist twice a year." Would you like to know what part of that formula has any value? Well...brushing after meals won't hurt you; of course. Using floss — *if* you know how and when —will definitely help you. *None* of the rest of the formula has any scientific or statistical meaning.

Seeing your dentist twice a year is beneficial only in that it helps the dentist pay his mortgages and support his social lifestyle; and in that you might come away with a "bi-annual prophylaxis" —a professional tooth cleaning that makes your smile pretty. This, in itself, is a considerable advantage to your *mental* health: Being socially acceptable, in our country, is psychologically a virtual necessity.

With a little training and an inexpensive device, you could do with the same prophylaxis whenever you wanted to, in the privacy of your bathroom, and it would satisfy the psychological/social requirements for "pretty teeth" and clean breath.

The other "benefit" of your trip to the dentist is that he can find out how much damage odontosis has done since your last trip; and he can then go to "work" with his bag of tricks to repair the damage (symptoms).

"Look, Ma...I only had one cavity!"

Super! If the kid is 12 years old, and he has only one cavity every six months, that's only two per year. At that rate, it will take 16 years for every tooth in his mouth to deteriorate from its healthy natural state to some sort of screwball mixture of "real" tooth with amalgam, bracing, splices, caps, and what have you...

If your car dealer told you that you had to come in every six months so he could repair breakdowns, would you buy that brand of automobile? Of course not!

If your medical doctor told you you have to check in every six months so that he can fine-tune your digestive tract, or operate on part of your body to get it back into condition...or replace knuckle bones...or whatever...you'd (quite properly) think he was crazy.

"Mrs. Wilson, you have a disease that eats away your kneecaps. Now, we know how to cure this disease; and we know how to prevent it, but I have a better idea. Why don't you just ignore it, and then come in every six months so I can operate on it and replace the damaged bone with plastic? By the time you're in your 40's, we will have totally replaced your real kneecaps with plastic. They won't work as well, but the disease will "peter out," because the germs don't eat plastic..."

(And, in the meantime, the doctor has realized thousands of dollars in clear profit.)

Of course, that example is clearly ridiculous...and of course no doctor would operate that way (at least, he wouldn't operate that way after the American Medical Association got wind of it.)

But that is *exactly* how your dentist views odontosis; and that is *exactly* how most Americans are convinced it "has to be." That is, also and unfortunately, *exactly* the approach to dentistry that is mandated by the dental associations and the state laws those associations have promulgated.

Oral hygiene is the most important aspect of continuing freedom from dental disease. There is no one single factor in the equation against disease that has as much bearing on your overall health, let alone on your dental health. Oral hygiene is first, last and always the core; the central and supremely important element of the cure/prevention of dental disease.

If dentists knew how to effect total oral hygiene (they don't); and if they knew how to teach patients the necessary methods (they don't), and if they had a means to psychologically "motivate" patients to perform the necessary hygiene (they never heard of motivation), and *if they would do it,* we would be looking at the last generation of dentists as the world knows them today.

If dentists were doing a medically sound "job," if they genuinely wanted to become doctors rather than repairmen, and if they were effective, they would be systematically working themselves out of an income, ...unless...they were willing to become preventive practitioners, medical dentists instead of mechanical dentists. Those professionals who practice Oramedics dentistry are realizing an income commensurate with their training, dedication and status as doctors: Why shouldn't they? They are treating disease; they are restoring health, their patients are paying less for more...there is no moral "wrong" in being paid for performance.

What we need to do, to understand oral hygiene, is to approach this subject with our old frame of reference discarded. We want you to take your "old" knowledge: "Brush after meals, use floss, avoid sweets, and see your dentist twice a year" —and put that knowledge where it belongs: In the trash-bin of history's obsolete "truths."

Let's start over.

Oral hygiene, to be effective, must begin with all the knowledge that very recent research can bring to bear. For a mind-blowing example, let's take the first paragraph of an article written in one of dentistry's most prestigious magazines, the *Journal of Preventive Dentistry,* in its May-June *1978* edition. That's this year; in fact it is so new that very few *dentists* will know of it...and certainly nobody in the general public.

The article begins:

"When a disease is poorly understood, generally, the most one can do for a patient is to repair the lesions (cavities) produced and alleviate any symptoms that may be present. At present, this is the predominant mode of treatment for dental caries, one of the most prevalent diseases in man. Now, through research, this situation is changing to one where the disease can either be prevented or its severity significantly reduced. Much of this is due to the sharp increase in knowledge about dental caries which has occured during the past decade. This has resulted in the development of new treatments, better use of known treatments..."

This kind of article is extremely rare in dental journals. To begin with, the information in such articles must be painfully gleaned from research papers from laboratories all over the world; then correlated and put together into a "whole" that makes sense.

The few publications which are beginning to tell dentistry some of the truths about dental disease are not drawn together in a way that a busy dentist can read and understand.

A dentist with any social conscience or professional pride, reading such an article, must come away with many conflicting thoughts and emotions. He would feel vaguely guilty because he'd know he wasn't practicing his profession as well as he could and should be. He would be slightly panic-stricken that there is a whole new area of research and information "out there" that he didn't get in dental school. And he would be very nervous: This sort of research sounds an awful lot like the mythical "pill" that will do away with dental disease —and dentists.

It will be very difficult for Oramedics doctors to resist saying, "we told you so" as these new approaches slowly become more and more familiar in the dental journals. In point of fact, Oramedics has been *trying* to "told you so" for two decades, now: The profession has resisted violently.

If Oramedics had any reason to hope that these new approaches will be assimilated by the profession, that they will bring significant changes, we would be more than elated. The fact that Oramedics doctors have been outcasts; have been punished and vilified for trying to bring these changes, would be forgiven instantly if the profession would only pay attention.

Oramedics doesn't care how the dentist learns to prevent disease...we just want him to learn it, *somehow.*

But we must be aware of the profession's dismal track record in this respect: Not all research in preventive dental medicine is within the past ten years. There have been leaders, pioneers, who have tried desperately to change the profession; some of them for generations.

Historically, this profession has responded to any change so slowly, so reluctantly, that there is little or no reason to hope that these new research advances will help you, or your children, or even your children's children, *unless the public forces the profession* to join the twentieth century *now.*

The education of the dentist must start with a new concept of oral hygiene. In this, he must be taught that oral hygiene is not a matter of "pearly whites." Nor is it a question of teaching a reluctant patient how to use dental floss: An exercise in futility, since the patient has no idea how important this is, or why —there is no reason to hope that he will do as his dentist says even if the dentist does take the time to explain it.

The dentist has to enter a strange new world: The world of the total oral environment. Oral hygiene must be understood as involving the pH content of the mouth (the acid/alkaline balance)...as involving the saliva function...as involving the presence/absence of *Lactobacullus acidophilus* and *Streptococcus mutans* germs...as involving the relationship of carbohydrates (diet) and the enzymatic production of the salivary glands...and on, and on, and on.

It isn't necessary that the *patient* become deeply involved in such research. In truth, much of it is pretty "deep" for people without some clinical education.

The patient must understand the practical aspects of the total oral environment...personal oral hygiene... and if we ever hope for people to actually practice effective hygiene, we *must realize* that people need to know "why" in addition to knowing "how" —or they simply will not have any motivation.

The dentist needs to *understand* statements like the following, taken from that same *Preventive Dentistry* article:

"Solubilization of the tooth translates into a function, the critical pH, which is that pH at which enough acid is present to exceed various protective mechanisms which influence the calcium phosphate solubility conditions in the tooth and plaque environment and thereby bring about loss of tooth mineral..."

The *patient* needs to understand that the balance of acid in his mouth is established by the presence or absence of plaque (how clean is the tooth?) and by the presence of microbes (Streptococcus and Lactobacillus germs), and by the sugars available for those germs to manufacture acid.

The dentist will have to "hit the books" until he understands about saliva; for example: "(saliva) facilitates clearance of carbohydrate substrates and their acidic products...neutralizes plaque acids by the buffers it contains, mainly bicarbonate; and most importantly, it contains nitrogenous substrates that are metabolized by the oral bacteria into basic products that neutralize the acid generated during carbohydrate breakdown..."

(Whew). We can let the dentist "chew" on propositions like that; and, once he understands them, he can translate them for his patients. What is important in that statement is that saliva —good old Mother Nature's all-purpose spit —is part of the oral environment's anti-disease squad. It is *vital* to oral health.

There is one statement in that quote that is interesting, in passing: What is that remark about carbohydrate acid being neutralized by a buffer...mainly bicarbonate? Sounds familiar, doesn't it? What is bicarbonate...? Isn't it that old, familiar yellow box of baking soda? It sure is! If that is a natural element of saliva, and if it's good to help fight cavities, was Grandma "on to" something when she used good old baking soda as a tooth powder?

Grandma was right. She may want to welcome the dental profession, now that "science" has caught up with her...

How can the importance of saliva have any bearing on my personal oral hygiene? I mean, it's good to know that spit helps keep my teeth healthy, but there isn't much I can do, personally, about my spit glands, is there?

There sure is! As you learn more and more how much emphasis Oramedics puts on whole-body health, you will begin to realize that oral health and physical health are totally inseparable.

Not that there is such a mystery in all of that, it's just that the public and the dental profession have, for generations, tried to separate oral health from whole-body health as if the mouth wasn't really part of the overall "system."

What has that got to do with saliva? If you are a drug addict, pay close attention. If you are overweight and your doctor is prescribing diet pills, pay careful attention. If you're having emotional problems and your doctor has you on tranquilizers, listen closely:

Amphetamines —diet pills, the addict's "uppers" and tranquilizers, which your teenager would instantly identify as "downers" —if you are taking either or both of these —are seriously impairing your dental health. The use of such medications immediately affects the ability of your salivary glands to function. There is a demonstrated increase in disease activity when such medications are used.

Does your doctor know that...?

Does your dentist know that...?

You know it, now; and that is how your own approach to personal oral hygiene has a relationship to the beneficial action of saliva in your mouth. If you *now* use such medications, or if a doctor prescribes them in the future, you will have to compensate for the decrease in saliva efficiency by using medication and methods we will explain later in this book.

Incidentally, if your doctor or dentist doesn't know about the relationship of amphetamines or tranquilizers to dental disease processes, ask him to write to Oramedics. We'll give him technical information he should be made aware of. It would be about time he learned...

Health enthusiasts often emphasize the benefits —the necessity —of cleansing and rejuvenating the body. To such people, the role played by saliva in a healthy mouth will not be a mystery at all, once they are made aware of it. Perhaps more than any other physical body function, saliva is Mother Nature's number one candidate for this role. Cleansing and rejuventating the mouth is a *primary* function of saliva; without it, there is no hope of controlling dental disease.

Oramedics research developed this relationship to whole-mouth hygiene years ago, when a few "stubborn" cases of odontosis seemed to cling beyond the point where effective hygiene had destroyed the disease in most people.

A careful analysis of diet, of medications consumed, and the relationship of saliva production in such persons resulted in an approach which works against dental disease even in what would ordinarily have been considered "hopeless" cases.

Some people may have chemical deficiencies in their saliva which need to be balanced medically. These cases are not usual, but they do happen. An Oramedics doctor (or any dentist who knew how, and wanted to) can have a laboratory analysis of the saliva conducted. The absence of the necessary nitrogenous materials, the peptides and tetrapeptides (notably Sialin) and other factors can be compensated for medically.

It should be noted that these chemicals are *naturally* present in healthy saliva; so the Oramedics doctor's prescribing them in deficiency cases is simply a matter of restoring a *natural* environmental balance. Compare this, for example, with medications which are effective against certain conditions, but which are not *natural* elements of the physical makeup.

Again: Health enthusiasts will not be the least surprised to discover that the introduction of unnatural medications ("speed" or "downers") into the system at one point (the blood stream) will result in degradation of natural function elsewhere (the saliva). This careful natural orchestration of whole-body, whole-health balance is something we upset only at great risk. Science almost daily discovers that what we do in one part of the system as a "remedy" often upsets something beneficial elsewhere in the system.

For this reason, the Oramedics approach constantly emphasizes using natural methods and natural systems to combat dental disease. There is no better way of preventing odontosis than to simply "help" the perfectly *natural* processes to do their job. Any other approach, any method which interferes with this finely-tuned ecological environment, may seem to work at first glance...but in the long run, it may do more harm than good.

Another important aspect of oral hygiene is the prevention of plaque formation. This is accomplished by cleaning properly; and sometimes must be enhanced by medication. It must always be considered in conjunction with diet.

Defeating oral germs doesn't necessarily mean wholesale elimination: It means, instead, that these germs are not allowed to colonize or to become organized. If they are present, but in disorganized state, our old friend saliva will constantly, gently wash them away.

There is a clinical test which will show, absolutely, the presence (or absence) of organized germs. This is called the "Lactobacillus saliva culture test" and it is something dentistry has known about for generations. Most dentists consider it an oddity; something of no value. In fact, there are very few laboratories in the U.S. that are set up to process saliva cultures for this purpose. There is a special research laboratory in Canton, Ohio: Established simply to meet the needs of Oramedics doctors who *insist* on Lacto. cultures as a necessary diagnostic tool in evaluating individual patient health.

This test will show the quantity of germs present in the mouth: If there are numbers of germs per milliliter of saliva over a certain percentage, there will be active odontosis. It doesn't matter how "clean" you *think* your mouth is: There will be odontosis if there are organized germs.

The dentist who gives you a six-month checkup, who fills a cavity and has his assistant give you a prophylaxis, may sincerely believe he has done his best for you. At any event, you would think so, wouldn't you?

In all truth, the dentist probably inoculated healthy teeth with colonized germs. This doctor-induced disease has a big Latin name, which makes doctors climb the wall: Iatrogenic disease is far more prevalent than doctors want us to know; it is far more prevalent than dentists will ever know.

Unless the dentist made sure, through testing and administration of medicines, that all of the active Strep. mutans and Lacto. were defeated during your trip to his office, the bugs were still there when you went to sleep that night. There were more of them the next night. Sooner or later, during the nighttime hours when saliva production tapers off, when there is more likelihood of mouth-breathing and the attendant dryness which decreases the natural bathing action of the mouth, those germs would find new homes and begin new cavities.

By the time you returned to the dentist six months later, there would be more symptom-damage for him to "fix" with his drill-spit-fill method. He'd have his assistant "shine 'em up" for you again, and give you a listless pep talk something like this: "Be sure you brush between meals, use floss, avoid sweets, and make an appointment to see me in six months..."

As you depart, he might turn to his assistant and remark, "Gee...I wish everybody took care of their teeth as well as he does..."

—Why wouldn't he wish that? He really enjoys, for a change, operating in a semi-clean mouth (you should see some of the cesspools he encounters); and he most certainly enjoys patients who visit (checkbook in hand) with clockwork regularity every six months for another "fix."

How do we, as individuals, fight the war against germs? The key —again, and again, and again —is that we must keep these germs from organizing into colonies. This can be partially accomplished medically ...through the use of a mouthrinse, one which requires a prescription and which we will discuss more fully in the section dealing with oral medicines.

Mostly, however, the fight against organized germs has to do with two things: Brushing the teeth and using dental tape. Your dentist will tell you that no toothbrush will reach all of the surface areas of your teeth —and he's 100% right.

The use of a secondary cleaning method is not just a "good idea" —it's absolutely essential. The secondary method Oramedics recommends is dental tape. Dental floss is also effective, but it is less effective; more difficult to use, and often causes cuts in gum tissue.

At this point, a brief reminder of what disease

germs like to do when they find an opening in the barrier tissue inside your mouth...they invade! Let's not cut this tissue with floss when there's another, better way to get the job done...dental tape.

There are other "gimmicks" that are also good: Toothpicks are helpful; as are some manufactured items (such as Stim-U-Dent, a trade-marked product available in most drugstores, used to help clean between teeth).

How often should you brush your teeth? —once an hour wouldn't hurt, would it? Is it enough to brush them after every meal? Sure it *is*, if you do it right...but that isn't really necessary; and it is sometimes inconvenient.

In a research study that lasted for more than two years, scientists proved absolutely that if the teeth were professionally cleaned *every two weeks* without *any* daily maintenance, there was no further disease activity. (As with all research mentioned in this book, the actual report is available upon request from Oramedics International).

We can prove that a total cleaning every two weeks is adequate to prevent dental disease...and we can also prove that brushing your teeth once an hour won't make the slightest difference.

What comes through, here, that makes any sense at all? Isn't it that it doesn't matter nearly as much how *often* you brush, as it does *how well you do it*?

Therein lies one of Oramedics deepest "secrets" —a secret we would like to shout from the housetops. Once people discover that how you clean your teeth makes a day-and-night difference; and then learn how to do it, we will have conquered dental disease in America.

The recommended frequency of brushing, for those in Oramedics therapy, is this: Brush as often as you can; preferably, if possible, brush after meals...but in any event, brush *once a day* before retiring. If you do this, and do it properly, you will have almost ensured freedom from dental disease. In fact, in the event for whatever reason you are unable to do this from time to time...if you miss a night here and there, but not often...it probably won't do you any harm.

The best method of brushing the teeth can be learned from a dentist (how *about* that?) or from any one of several publications for self-teaching. Oramedics, of course, has such materials available: In fact, there is a ''system'' approach to this which combines a written publication keyed to a recorded cassette tape.

We can't, in the scope of this book, give instructions on the proper method of toothbrushing. This information is available, from a number of different sources; and if you continue to have any difficulty finding it, write Oramedics. The important thing —the vital thing —is that you recognize the *fact* that you are not presently able to properly brush your teeth because nobody ever told you (1) your health *depends* on it and (2) how to do it, and (3) why.

Again...this information is relatively easy to find. If any of this book has made any sense to you at all, up to this point, then please pay attention to the following paragraph:

It is *your* responsibility to learn how to brush your teeth properly, and it is *your* responsibility to do it. If you aren't motivated enough at this point, or at least after you've digested this material, it is unlikely that you will overcome the inertia and make the effort. That would be tragic, because your health hangs in the balance. In fact, if you truly don't intend to follow through with this one part of what you've learned, there's no reason to finish this book...why not give it or sell it to someone who might benefit from it?

Frequently people are surprised and momentarily upset when Oramedics doctors find it necessary to ''jack them up'' for not performing personal hygiene, after they've been taught how. It is a total departure from the ''normal'' dental attitude, but it would be not at all unusual in a medical doctor's office.

Consider: If there was some health problem which made it necessary for you to seek medical treatment, and the doctor made it your responsibility to do something —or avoid something —as part of his therapy, how long would he let you "get away" with ignoring his instructions?

It wouldn't be the least bit unusual for an M.D. to tell a patient, "Look! I've *told* you how important this is to your health; now, if you don't intend to follow my advice, don't bother coming back here!"

The same attitude in a dentist's office would be strange, indeed. For one thing, how many dentists would willingly tell a once-every-six-month "meal ticket" to not come back? For another...without clinical procedures, the dentist has no way of knowing whether the patient is doing his oral hygiene properly. Remember...the average dentist is just as locked in to the incorrect attitude that dental disease is inevitable as you once were.

"Only one cavity" may be good news in a conventional dentist's office, but it would be cause for alarm and concern in an Oramedics practice.

That's why, if an Oramedics patient comes to one or two appointments and "flunks" his saliva test and/or his Navy Plaque Index examination, the doctor is critically interested in discovering why: Is it something in the diet? Is there a physio/chemical imbalance in the saliva? Is the patient on some other medications that affect oral health?

If the answers to none of these bring any light; the patient will be closely questioned as to his oral hygiene habits. Should it turn out that he is "fudging," that he either doesn't understand or doesn't care how important his "half" of the doctor-patient relationship really is, he will hear something very similar to what he'd hear in an M.D.'s office:

"Look, Mr. Smith...if you don't intend to help us help you, you might as well realize that you are wasting your money and my time. Your teeth are going to have problems and, frankly, we don't prefer to do mechanical dentistry here. Maybe you'd be more realistic if you gave this some thought before you come back again..."

This is not usually the case, however, with Oramedics patients. Ordinarily, they understand their end of the doctor-patient relationship and are very happy that somebody finally made sense to them about their oral health.

What usually happens with an Oramedics "checkup" is that the patient passes the Lacto. count and N.P.I. test with flying colors; for which he is given a merit badge to sew on his jacket (no kidding!); a thorough cosmetic cleaning of his teeth (to make them truly "pearly-whites"), another appointment for six months to a year away...and an invoice that says: "Congratulations! Zero disease activity...and no charge."

—That's right. When Oramedics patients achieve and maintain zero disease levels, they don't pay a cent for their "checkups" —and, of course, they don't need any "fixing" dentistry, anyway.

The next part of personal oral hygiene, then, is the use of dental tape. This is available in almost any drugstore; Oramedics also manufactures its own "brand" named "Clean-Between." Dental tape is wider than floss, and it is waxed. It is used in the same way as floss but there is far less potential for "snapping" the tape between tightly-adjacent teeth and thereby cutting the gum tissue.

Because tape is wider, it is also easier to handle with the fingers and obviously covers a larger surface area of the tooth. The use of such tape in conjunction with the once-nightly thorough brushing is the "other half" of personally-administered hygiene.

Most people complain that they "don't have time" to do this thorough dental taping. It is probably a telling symptom of our hurry-up society that so many people are unwilling to spend five or ten minutes a

night, even when they know it might mean the difference between health and sickness, to care for their
teeth.

But that isn't important. What is important is
that you find the time. Notice: We don't suggest that
you "take the time" or "make the time" —instead,
that you "find" the time. One of the more interesting
things we've discovered is the surprised reaction
people have to our frequent suggestion:

"Mr. Smith, how much time do you and your
family spend watching the TV in the evening?"

"Oh, I dunno...coupla hours, I guess. Why?"

"Do you know that you could be using dental tape
for that whole time without interfering with your TV
program in the slightest? You don't have to stand in
front of your bathroom mirror to do it..."

One woman wrote Oramedics a letter, saying that
she used to sit with her family of an evening, watching
TV and "taping" her youngest child's teeth, his head
cradled in her lap. When he grew a little bit older, he
said, "Mommy...let me try that..."

She helped him learn to do it for himself and he
naturally continued the habit of taping his teeth while
watching TV.

That was over eighteen years ago: The child is
now grown into a strapping young man. He has all of
his second teeth in a perfectly healthy mouth; no
fillings, no artificial appliances...nothing but natural,
shining teeth. He has had a lifetime of zero dental
disease.

And neither his parents nor himself have ever
spent one cent at the dentist's office for his care.

Think about it.

That same woman told us that when she first heard
about Oramedics she was dubious: She didn't really
believe that anyone could actually prevent dental
disease. However, she and her family "signed up"
those long years ago; and she today cheerfully tells
anyone who is interested that Oramedics has made her

whole family healthier.

Think about it: What if all your children grew from infancy to adulthood without a single dental problem; and it never cost you a dime for any of them...?

As with brushing, there is a right way and a wrong way to use floss or tape. Again, the methods are not difficult to learn and the information is easily available.

You might also want to buy some "disclosing tablets" at your drugstore. These tablets are a natural food dye; you chew them after brushing and flossing and then check in your mirror. The dye will wash right off clean, healthy teeth: A quick rinse with water will get the dye out of your mouth.

Any areas you "missed" with the brush or tape; anyplace in the mouth where there is plaque formed ...even if you couldn't have seen the plaque with your unaided eye...the dye will adhere. These plainly-marked areas can then be given a "second lick" and, when the dye is thus removed...so is the plaque.

While this is a very good visual indicator for adults, to make sure the cleaning is thorough, it is a superb training aid for youngsters, helping them develop consistent, effective hygiene methods. They consider it "fun" to use, also...the glaring orange or purple color of the dye occasions many giggles and "monster-faces" in the mirror. What better way to get a child involved in "cleansing and rejuvenating" his mouth?

While we're on the subject of brushing and taping, we should mention the various cleaning materials on the market. Is it better to use Superstuff Toothpaste, fortified with Zap-14 and Freebistan; or should you use ShineBrite, the toothpaste of TV stars...or would you be better off with Doctor Zinger's Miracle-White; the toothpaste advocated by the American Theatre Guild, the American Dental Society, Ringling Brothers and P.T. Barnum?

—Use something more than just plain water, if

you have it readily available. If not...just go ahead and brush; even if you don't have water. Mother Nature put a bunch of little water fountains in your mouth, anyway. But don't be overly concerned about which toothpaste is best. You might as well just buy whatever is on sale, if you're a "toothpaste" family. You'd be far better off with tooth powder; one of the old fashioned kind: There are many on the shelves, and they are much cheaper than toothpaste...and they work better. You'd be hard-pressed to come up with a better toothpaste, as a matter of fact, than Grandma's old standby: Good old baking soda. It works just fine.

How about fluoride toothpastes? —Well; fluoride is definitely a plus for healthy teeth. Later in this book, when we discuss oral medicines, we'll have much more to say about fluoride. For now, however: Yes, fluoride in toothpaste is a good idea; if it's used properly, it certainly won't harm you and it can do a certain amount of good. It has been clinically proven to be *partially* effective in controlling incidence of caries: In other words, in an unhealthy mouth, fluoride in toothpaste is a whole lot better than nothing.

If you do use fluoridated toothpaste, please don't expect it to do more than it can. In this sense, such preparations may have the same effect as fluoride in the public water supply: They are *marginally* effective; they can help and sometimes they do help, but they *do not* substitute for proper oral hygiene and maintenance of the whole oral environment.

If you use fluoridated products or water supplies as a substitute for your parental responsibility to supervise your children's oral health, you are doing them a grave disservice.

In short: Use fluoridated products if you wish, to bolster your overall hygiene, but do not let the use of these products lull you into a false sense of security. Fluoridated products that you can use or buy without a doctor's prescription are simply not effective against dental disease without the accompanying personal hygiene and a coordinated program to combat the causes of disease.

Oral hygiene is the backbone of any preventive program. What you do, and how you do it, is directly related to your oral health as no other part of the overall therapy can be.

The doctor can help you with clinical tests, with diet recommendations and, if need be, through prescribing rinses or other preparations. He can give you instruction and encouragement if you need it.

But no doctor can come home with you each night, and gently chide you until you've given your teeth a thorough brushing; until you've used dental tape between the teeth.

Perhaps the best way of saying this is to point out that it is highly unlikely that you can eliminate dental disease without at least some help from the doctor ...but, given the knowledge of this book and perhaps a few more facts gained from U.S. Government or Oramedics publications; and with some through-the-mail tests that you can obtain, you *could* do it without the doctor's immediate help. On the other hand, there is no way...and no doctor...to achieve freedom from dental disease *without* your help. In this doctor-patient relationship, the final result is squarely up to you.

Chapter Seven
The Power to Heal

We've briefly mentioned, earlier, that teeth can often heal themselves. Overwhelming research, conducted within the past decade, has reached this conclusion to the point that it can no longer be seriously challenged. As a matter of fact, we now know that even damaged jawbone can be restored —can heal itself —provided the environment is condusive to natural healing.

This raises a question: "If teeth and oral bone can heal itself...if recent research evidence forces this conclusion...why hasn't the profession reported this phenomena before now? Why has everyone simply gone along with the "knowledge" that there is no return for damaged oral bone and tissue?

There's no pat answer to that question. The answer probably lies in philosophy: Many reports on current research will begin with a lead-in sentence something like this: "Until now, members of the profession have assumed..." or "Before the conclusion of recent research, there has been no awareness within the profession that..."

It seems likely that the profession has not known about these things because they were "blinded" by the frame of reference which is based on the belief that dental disease is inevitable, incurable and not-preventable. The isolated incidences of natural restoration (healing) would be written off by individual doctors as "flukes;" therefore not consistently reported in professional journals, etc.

For example: There is a phenomena well known to any practicing dentist; known as the Brown Spot Lesion. This is a portion of enamel which is discolored and which shows evidence of earlier carious activity —a cavity had begun to form. Somehow, without medical assistance, the cavity formation was arrested and the re-surfaced enamel was different from the original white enamel. Recent studies show that the restored enamel, besides being a different color, is *much more resistant* to future carious attacks. Not only did the tooth "heal" —it developed an immunity!

Brown Spot Lesions have been observed, as a dental oddity, for decades. Only recently has concentrated research uncovered the astonishing reality: This is evidence of the mouth's toughness, its ability to adapt, to function and even to protect itself *in spite of* disease.

There is one consistent thread running through all contemporary research which underlines natural healing: In every case, the research was set up so that disease was *controlled* —and then the healings took place.

"In an environment where the Lactobacillus count was maintained below a level of..." or "The control group recieved no prophylaxis, the test group received prophylaxis on a bi-weekly basis, with the result that..."

When these researchers set up actual, long-range tests, and *eliminate odontosis,* they report again and again that teeth, bone and tissue can heal itself.

What makes teeth, bone and tissue able to fight off disease; or to actually restore itself in the continued absence of disease? Now that the profession has been put on notice that these things can and will happen, how will dentists respond to this?

It will be many years before this research filters down through the profession, through the dental schools, and into the offices where the profession meets the public in a one-on-one relationship. Until that begins to happen, these facts will have no bearing on dentistry whatever.

Oramedics doctors, who were aware of such results long before scientific research produced the "why" it happens, have been sharply criticized for trying to introduce such "heresy" at the practical level of dentistry. Even though thousands of Oramedics case

67

histories proved (empirically) that teeth can heal in the absence of disease, it has been only during the past ten years that Oramedics International could point to scientific research that backed up the empirical success with documented, acceptable science.

Oramedics publications such as "What Makes Johnny Run?" (an overview of what's wrong with American Dentistry) and "Research Advocates Oramedics" (research documentation underlining Oramedics theory and practice) have drawn blistering retribution from organized dentistry.

The essence of all of this is that change, if it comes at all, will come very slowly at the practical levels... at the firing line of dentistry. Until the dentist in private practice becomes convinced that his own clients will no longer settle for "drill, spit and fill" mechanical dentistry, he has no reason to change; especially when his own associations are fighting it!

And so, once again, it becomes at least partly your responsibility to know the facts...even if reading some of this is dry and unexciting. If you want to have enough mental ammunition to go up against a conventional dentist and force him to *think,* you'll need to have a fairly secure understanding of how oral bone and tissue can heal itself (with a little help from medical dentistry).

We've mentioned before that the teeth are far and away the toughest part of the human body. Given any chance at all, these 32 pearly-whites should outlast the rest of the "system" —when the ticker finally quits pumping; when the arteries have gotten so hardened and brittle the body begins to falter; the teeth *should* be alive and well.

The same goes for gum tissue, oral bone and...yes ...even the relatively-fragile connective tissue. Given a fighting chance, all of these will outlast the human lifetime.

What is the fighting chance they need? They need to be in an environment free from dental disease

—there must be *no* odontosis active in the oral ecology. If we can provide such an environment, Mother Nature will do the rest.

Oramedics developed its oral health care "system" by observing, to a large extent, the natural forces in the oral ecology. Long before public awareness of "natural health" became an organized movement in this country, it was already apparent that in all branches of health care the most effective approaches were those that most closely approximated the natural order of things.

Restated: When medicine introduces synthetic, abnormal or un-natural elements into the whole-body system, there are usually undesirable side effects.

In some cases, the side effects were better than the disease; more tolerable. An early example of this is, of course, the use of arsenic —a deadly poison —in controlled, long-term dosages, as a medical response to syphilis. It usually worked, after a long period. Of course, the poison raised havoc with the health; but not so much as the disease would have, given free reign.

As science accelerated its research, its response to human disease, we learned that the best "cures" were those that imitated natural defenses as closely as possible. We discovered antibodies, for example: The ability of natural defenses to create systemic responses to specific disease organisms. Anthrax was a dread disease until science discovered how the body tries to fight it: Then we learned how to produce a serum which could "trigger" the body's production of antibodies. When such medicines were administered, the natural ability of the body was augmented a thousand-fold; but in a manner consistent with the *natural* order. Almost always, it worked; and usually without adverse side-effects.

Somewhere on one of your arms, probably high up on the shoulder, there's a small, round scar. You've had it so long you ignore it: If you see one on a cute lady in a bathing suit, you ignore it. Everybody has one, these days: It's perfectly "natural," in our society.

Because you have that scar, you've never had smallpox. In fact, you'd have to stop and think to remember what smallpox is all about. *Nobody* gets smallpox anymore. Why? —Because everybody gets an immunization early in life. The immunization, of course, is a scientific enhancement of the natural ability to reject smallpox causing microorganisms.

The entire physical/mental system we call the body and mind demonstrates, over and over again, that its *natural* function is to keep itself clean; to get rid of waste, to constantly fine-tune its chemical balance, to replace damaged bone and tissue —often with bone and tissue superior to the original. You might very well say that the natural "attitude" of the human body is to fight, with everything it has, to stay healthy; to restore and rejuvenate itself.

For generations, however, there was a weird frame of reference that said, "these truths don't apply to the mouth and teeth." The overwhelming evidence everywhere else in the body was in favor of natural healing; but nobody believed the mouth was "part of the system." Public and profession alike thought of dental "things" as being exempt from the natural order. It was as though the whole of society had simply given up hope; our mouths were, somehow, out of nature's control and therefore beyond anything we could do against disease.

About twenty years ago a young dentist saw this frame of reference; became aware of the wholesale illogic of this position, and, in effect, said: "That's incredible! *I don't believe it!*" —And Oramedics was born.

How he managed to shake off the years of conditioning in dental school; how he was able to reach novel conclusions independently of his professional societies and colleagues, how he was able to approach his innovative research and practice all alone and not "cave in" to self-doubt and isolation...these are, perhaps, the sort of mystery that history calls "insight" once a major medical milepost is reached and an important corner in history is turned.

For years, as he became more and more a "force to reckon with," the professional societies fought back harder and harder. To this day, he is a pariah to the hallowed superstructure of organized dentistry. For many years, his theories could be proved only by looking at his hundreds —and then thousands —of case histories. Oramedics *worked*; his clients knew it: Whole families were free of dental disease. He lectured, he traveled first nationwide and then in many foreign countries; always "preaching" the "gospel" of preventive medical dentistry...in the sense that the word gospel translates into the English language as "good news."

Why are we telling you all of this? Because you must know, for your own benefit, that organized dentistry is *still* trying to discredit this doctor, and Oramedics. If and when you become an Oramedics-oriented, prevention-oriented patient, you will discover that the profession will fight back, and fight back hard, against some of the things you're learning.

For years all that kept Oramedics "alive" was one doctor's determination and insight; all Oramedics had going for it was case histories that empirically showed Oramedics could stop dental disease in its tracks...and keep it stopped.

Only within the past ten years, fifteen at the most, has research begun to produce the clinical, laboratory proofs that underline so many long-time Oramedics approaches. For years, we could prove that our methods *worked*; but when the profession demanded chapter and verse on *why* they worked, we were at a disadvantage.

Now, more and more, we can point to laboratory work at this university, or that dental college, or some

other research center, and say, *"That's* why it works!"
But it will be many years before this knowledge is
assimilated by a profession that is fighting against it;
and so you should know that if this new research is to
be of any benefit to you personally, or your family,
you will have to join our growing band of people who,
like Dr. Nara years ago, are willing to set yourself
stubbornly in place against the "truth" the profession
is trying to peddle and say, "But that's incredible!
I don't believe it!"

Let's look at some of the natural defenses; some of
the natural restorative abilities of the mouth. We have
already discovered together the slightly surprising
importance of saliva. It does much more than help a
youngster make spitballs on a lazy autumn school day.
It is the mouth's sanitary system, its lubricating
system. It is a major partner, along with the teeth, in
the preparation of food for healthy digestion.

What else does it do? How does saliva *naturally*
help combat disease and restore damaged tissue and
bone? Once we understand how nature gives saliva
"the power to heal," we can augment this power
medically. Without introducing something foreign to
the ecology; or at least without ingesting chemicals
which can upset some other part of the overall, whole-
body system, we can temporarily vastly enhance the
natural process.

We don't fight against nature, we fight *with* it:
Knowing that nature can heal, we simply advance the
logical conclusion that nature can heal faster with a
"little help from its friends."

Earlier we noted that there is a direct relationship
between the pH balance and carious activity in the
mouth. Once the level of acid becomes critical, there is
significant danger of cavities.

We already know that this acid is produced by
germs working on sugar and producing acid. Of
course, that is why the dental profession is so paranoid
about our "avoiding sweets." Later on, we will give

you scientific proof that you're better off eating caramel candy than white bread...but that's another story.

For now, let's just observe the logical, plain truth: There is *no way* you can avoid sugar in your mouth: Sugar can form from carbohydrates...honey... raw sugar...from protein...from so many foods that, if you actually want to avoid sugar, you'll have a super-human task ahead of you.

There "ain't no such animal" as a sugar-free diet. Obviously, the most sensible approach is to control the germs, since we are not ever going to totally control the sugar.

So...enter saliva. "In humans," says the *Journal of Preventive Dentistry,* "the plaque pH decreases more following a sucrose rinse when access of the saliva to the plaque bacteria is restricted than when saliva is allowed free access."

Translation: Sugar in a diseased environment *immediately* begins acid production, but it decreases more rapidly when saliva is introduced than it would without saliva.

Why?

There is, of course, the washing action itself; helping to remove the sugar from the area, also moving numbers of the free-floating bacteria themselves... the germs that aren't firmly entrenched in the plaque film, in organized colonies.

But there's more to saliva than just water and salt, the saline solution we usually think of in connection with physical fluids. There is bicarbonate, there are nitrogenous substrates which produce ammonia (urea is the most prominent of these substrates); there are basic peptides containing arginine, which yield amines and ammonia. A very recent discovery is the presence of a tetrapeptide named Sialin: This chemical has the capacity of returning acid levels rapidly to safe or normal after the introduction of sugar.

Saliva also contains calcium and phosphate. This is both good news and bad news. It's very good news in a mouth without disease-producing organisms; a mouth free from plaque. It's bad news to those whose oral environment favors odontosis. The calcium and phosphate in saliva helps create calculus and tartar ...the precursors to gingivosis and odontosis...in a diseased environment.

However, when there is no plaque-forming disease, this same calcium and phosphate present in saliva gives the tooth enamel a constant "bath" of the very elements which make up tooth enamel. It is this availability of the building blocks which results, in the absence of disease, in the "healing" of initial carious lesions: It is very highly probable that this is how Mother Nature creates those Brown Spot Lesions we have discovered are probably naturally-healed cavities.

We're going to quote from research data directly about this calcium and phosphate; with our apologies in advance for it's being "heavy." There are two parts of this clinical language we want you to read as the research report stated it; after which we'll take a look again in plain language. Here goes:

The calcium and phosphate are present in saliva in two forms. One is as ions; as such they can retard, by mass action, the loss of similar ions from the tooth. The other is in the form of an amorphous or poorly crystalline calcium phosphate bound to carbohydrate protein. This material is deposited from saliva during plaque formation and is readily solubilized and available as a substitute for enamel hydroxyapatite in preventing development of a caries lesion.

What we want to observe from this is that, number one, there is an ion —submicroscopic particle —of the "building block" or tooth enamel available in saliva. This constant bathing of the tooth with this atomically-adhesive ion continually replaces the same material lost from the tooth surface. Did you ever wonder why tooth enamel doesn't just simply "wear out" over the years? —It might, mightn't it, if it wasn't constantly rebuilt through something far, far too exotic for a typical dentist: Ion exchange. A physicist would have no trouble understanding this.

The second thing to observe is that "something" in the saliva actually combines with plaque...with one of the major disease mechanisms...to help fight cavities. Mother Nature continues to amaze and delight researchers: In this case, the natural elements in saliva infiltrate disease-causing plaque and, from within, "is...available as a substitute for enamel...in preventing development of a caries lesion."

Science has not, as yet, developed vehicles for direct use of these basic chemicals in saliva. For example, Sialin seems to head the list of naturally-produced disease/acid fighters. When and if science finds a vehicle...a rinse, a chewing gum...whatever... with which Sialin can be augmented, can be elevated far above its "natural" quantity...we will have added a powerful weapon in our arsenal against odontosis.

There is one chemical we now have; one upon which there has been research and practical experience for years and years. That chemical is one of the least understood by the public; one of the most-maligned and most controversial "medicines" we have today. What is it? Of course, it is fluoride: Let's talk about it.

To begin with, fluoride is not a "natural" chemical. You won't find it in saliva or anywhere else in the body, except for perhaps some "accidental" traces.

Fluoride is one of those discoveries that people used because it worked; even before they really had a handle on *why* it worked. There are a number of different formulations of fluoride that have been used, and in a variety of ways.

We've put fluoride into toothpaste and into the public water supply. We've used it in a method your dentist calls "topical application," which simply means that someone in the dentist's office —or a person licensed to do it in school —painted it onto the teeth, or swabbed it onto the teeth, or used a cleaning agent that was laced with fluoride.

We've made pills you can take which introduce fluoride into the system, by which the chemical ultimately finds its way into the oral ecology.

This ingested fluoride —pills and drinking water —is responsible for the bad reputation which "turns off" many people when they hear about this chemical. Is it an infringement on personal freedom when fluoride is put into the drinking water...so that you can't avoid it, like it or not? Do we know enough about the effects of fluoride on the human system apart from its benefit as a dental disease fighter?

We aren't going to try to answer either question now, because all the facts aren't in as yet. The one is a social question —does the government have the right to impose a chemical upon us? The other is a scientific question: What harm can fluoride engender over the long haul? We simply don't know the answer, yet, to the latter question; and the first question is for debate among philosophers: It is a matter of human rights, and not a matter of medical determination.

Oramedics views both of these questions as academic from the viewpoint of oral medicine, because ingestion of fluoride is the *least beneficial use,* and the use most subject to criticism. Why on earth, we wonder, does the profession insist on ramming a square peg into a round hole?

It can be demonstrated scientifically that fluorides in the water supply will lessen the incidence of dental caries in the young. Sure: There can't be any reasonable dispute to that; it can be proved, it's a fact.

Our contention is that a slight reduction in dental disease...only enough to be statistically significant... is *just not enough* when we are talking about a disease that can be totally and absolutely prevented. Why settle for "a little bit better" when you can more easily have the best there is?

76

We ask: What sense is there in misusing an effective medicine in such a way that it creates social tension; possible (though yet unproven) bad side-effects, and simply isn't genuinely efficient in producing the hoped-for result?

Any fluoride that is available today without a prescription and a doctor's supervision is simply not strong enough to do enough good for the teeth...and we have no way of proving that it won't do harm elsewhere in the system.

Why?

Fluoride is poison, that's why. In dosages of, say, one-fourth of one percent sodium fluoride solution, if you swallowed several ounces it would very probably kill you.

And yet, it is today the most efficient, effective disease-fighter dental science has discovered. As we learn more and more about the "why" fluoride works, this one chemical seems to have an astonishing affinity for constructive elements that are naturally present in the mouth. Even during this decade, researchers are saying, in effect, "we don't know exactly *how* fluoride works, but here's what it *does...*" —and then they go on to describe the beneficial effects of this chemical in warding off dental disease, and in helping the natural healing processes to accelerate.

Fluoride has been proven to dynamically accelerate the restoration of enamel surfaces; to help teeth heal early cavities.

Fluoride has been proven to help inhibit the incidence of cavities: It forms an atomic-structural bond with elements of the enamel and makes the natural germ fighting ability much stronger.

Fluoride has been proven to change the elementary makeup of enamel —its very molecular structure —to make it tougher.

Now, in 1978, comes still another "fluoride first:" Remember the earlier mention of the saliva component, Sialin? That natural chemical works to

77

neutralize the acids produced by germs.

Now, according to a recent article in the *Journal of Preventive Dentistry,* fluoride has been shown to work in a complementary manner with the natural effect of Sialin. Working together, these two chemicals ...one of them produced naturally within the mouth, the other a medicine introduced medically...are not only compatible, they are a team.

Fluoride is also a germicide: It is sudden death to Strep. mutans and Lacto. It has an "affinity" for bonding itself molecularly into plaque, tartar and calculus as well as natural enamel. Once bonded into place, it not only hardens enamel and enhances restoration, it continues to make these areas unsafe for habitation by germ-bearing microbes.

It is truly astonishing how this "unnatural" chemical seems to fit in, to mesh so well, with the natural functions of oral environment. If there was some way to use it so that all of its possible bad effects could be done away with, it might well be the wonder drug of oral medicine.

Well, it is...and there is a way. By diagnosing the specific requirements of an individual patient, the medical dentist can prescribe the proper dosage; the most efficient percentage of solution, in which to use sodium fluoride in a *mouthrinse.* The instructions on the child-proof bottle clearly state that you are to rinse with a tablespoonful, for sixty seconds, then spit it out and rinse the mouth with water. The chemical *is not* ingested.

During the sixty-second rinse at least two things happen: First, when that concentrated blast of sodium fluoride hits the germs, they curl up and die. Wham!

Second, during that one-minute rinse the atomic structure of the fluoride will "mesh" with the atomic structure of tooth enamel, calculus, tartar and plaque. What results won't be fluoride, anymore...nor will it be the same "other stuff," either. The enamel, plaque, calculus and tartar might *seem* to be the same, but they are different in one highly-significant respect:

They are now even more capable of bringing all their natural germ-and-disease fighting ability, all of their restorative and healing ability, into full production.

Of course, all you'll feel during this process is the "tingle" of the rinse's flavoring, the freshness of the mild astringent that is part of the formula; the "cleansing and rejuvenating" feeling of having the rinse cut through the mucous, food particles and debris of the oral cavity, leaving your mouth "sparkling clean," your breath naturally fresh and your teeth supernaturally strong.

Meanwhile, the "bad" aspect of sodium fluoride —the fact that, in your system, it is a poison —is on its way down the drain.

By now, you've read far enough in this book to be able to come up with an answer to the question: "If fluoride rinses are that effective, why don't more dentists encourage their use? Why doesn't the national association launch a massive public campaign to tell the public about fluoride *rinse* instead of trying to get fluoridated water supplies everywhere?

You could probably answer that question on your own, but we'd like to propose, by way of answering it, another question; after making a simple statement of fact:

Coupled with proper oral hygiene, fluoride rinses can absolutely eradicate dental disease...continued personal hygiene and, perhaps, occasional use of a fluoride rinse can absolutely prevent a recurrence.

The question: If you were making 30,000 to 50,000 dollars a year busily repairing or replacing the symptoms of disease damage, would you be likely to recommend the use of a preparation that could eliminate the disease?

What we are seeing, today, is a direct confrontation with the power of entrenched interests, of multibillion-dollar industries, up against another power:

One that the American Public deserves to know about, the sooner the better.

Avarice, greed and self-interest will always be with us...unfortunately, this seems to be part of the "normal" human condition. There's something else, however, that's also normal and natural: The power to heal.

Something has to give. Which way would you want it?

Chapter Eight
"Let Them Eat Cake..."

Do you recognize the quotation in this chapter subtitle? When, according to the historical account, French Queen Marie Antoinette was told that common folks were complaining that they had no bread; she is supposed to have remarked, "Then let them eat cake."

If true, that was a cruel irony: Suggesting that a rich man's luxury could substitute for a poor man's staff of life. Oddly enough, if it had been possible to make that substitution —or if it were made today —chances are that the dental associations would complain about the highly-refined sugars in the cake as detrimental to oral health.

Wrong...

Which of the two items are better for your dental health: (1) caramel candy, or (2) white bread?

If you've been paying attention in earlier chapters, we've already tipped you off that the candy is the least detrimental of the two. You probably got the answer right...without really knowing why. In order to increase your knowledge about total oral health, this chapter will discuss food and its direct relationship to dental disease. We're going to find out "why."

Once and for all, and hopefully forever, let's get rid of that old, hack saying, "avoid sweets." Horse manure! There is *no way* to "avoid sweets," and you know it, and so does your dentist. Everybody in the profession has known for generations that there's a direct link between sugar and dental disease: When high concentrations of sugar are present —frequently —there will be more disease damage than if lower concentrations were observed.

Based on that, the profession has loudly cried out against "sweets" for years and years. When was the last time you read this advice; or heard your dentist say it: "Avoid *germs*"? In the total absence of sugars, the germs will "lie low" —why not? They are starving!

But —there's no such thing as a total absence of sugars. If you "avoid sweets," those germs will take *other* food and *manufacture* sugar. They're tough bugs; nature has programmed some pretty good "survival" components into their invisible little hides.

If you are a master at self control, and have a college degree in nutrition, and enough money to be very highly selective in your food intake, you *might* be able to "avoid sweets" well enough to *reduce* disease damage. Is that a good idea? Ask an M.D. what he thinks of masking symptoms while leaving an active disease-producing mechanism in place. That would be about the equivalent of prescribing only enough penicillin to make a virulent disease "lie low," dormant, in your system. You may not feel or see the symptoms, but you sure haven't corrected the cause ...the disease itself.

However, since you can't probably reduce your sugar intake enough to starve the disease into total remission, look at it from the other side; the logical, rational side:

Without sugar, the germs don't do *quite as much* damage.

Without germs, the sugar won't do *any* damage.

—Which makes the most sense?

Oramedics has no simple (childish) catch phrase regarding sugar. We have no dogma to replace the asinine, "avoid sweets." We don't think our patients are so childish they cannot grasp, and remember, a whole concept instead of a two-word doggerel.

The active disease-enhancing element we want to limit (besides germs, of course) is basic sugar; which your body can manufacture from a long list of foods: Candy, carbohydrates (bread), protein (many items), starch (potatoes, bread, others) —and more.

There are two sensible ways to limit oral exposure to sugar. One of these is to be selective about what kind of foods you eat; the other is to be reasonable about how long you retain certain foods in your mouth.

82

Take hard candy, for instance: the "rock" candy so visible around Christmastime. The way most people eat this kind of candy is to pop one in the mouth and then suck on it until it's gone...many, many minutes. If you eat one after the other, you are actually bathing the oral cavity in raw sugar for long periods of time.

If there are any active disease germs in there, they'll think they went to heaven. How will they show their gratitude for this sweetness? —They'll manufacture acid, of course...like there's no tomorrow. What will the acid do? Mother was right, although she didn't quite have it all figured out: "Candy'll rot yer teeth."

Let's look at another "candy:" The sugar-coated breakfast foods our TV sets are busy hustling to our children. What about these?

Number one: The food is ingested, chewed, and swallowed. Most of the sugar goes "down the pipe." In comparison to sugars retained in the mouth, this is obviously not as dangerous, is it?

Number two: If you don't let your children eat pre-sweetened Zippidoos; insisting instead that they eat something that's "good for you," you will have to put a sugar bowl and spoon in front of them...they sure won't eat Health Flakes without *something* to flavor it!

Did you ever watch your kid ladle sugar onto breakfast food? (Did you ever watch *yourself?*) —So, as between non-sweetened and pre-sweetened foods, what have you really accomplished?

Number three: Research shows that this kind of sugar, ingested in this manner, is far *less* detrimental than the sugar contained in foods you've always assumed were "safe." That same research, incidentally, pointed out that offering children breakfast foods they enjoyed was one good way to get them to ingest more milk: A calcium-protein bearing food that has been proven beneficial to natural development and maintenance of tooth enamel.

What we want you to do, as far as your own

intake of sugar and that of your family, is to apply some basic logic, consider a few ground-rules, and then...enjoy your meal; including dessert if it turns you on.

There are two basic considerations related to the dietary/nutritional aspects of sugar. One, of course, is the effect of sugar on the whole-body health: We are not going to discuss that in a book about oral health except to mention a few brief items:

—Too much sugar will make you fat.

—Too much sugar will, eventually, help induce other very serious complications...ask your M.D.

—Too much sugar will throw your appetite and your food-selectivity into a cocked hat: You could get fat while starving to death.

There isn't any disagreement: Too much sugar is bad for you...period.

The aspect of sugar that we want to discuss a bit more carefully, here, is how it directly relates to oral health.

We've shown you the relationship of sugar and active odontosis. If the disease is present, the germs will use sugar to make acid. That will cause dental damage —symptoms.

We've indicated that the critical factor is not *how much* sugar is present, for example, but *for how long.*

We've mentioned that saliva is necessary to counteract the presence of sugar, in two ways: It constantly washes the mouth, dumping excess sugar down the hatch; and it contains chemicals that help reduce both the level of sugar and acid. Interestingly enough, one of the chemicals in saliva (Sialin) is ingested by the germs along with the sugar and tends to modify the germs' by-product: It actually "tells" the germs to stop making acid!

We've also mentioned that some chemical balances in the whole-body system can dynamically upset both the amount of saliva the body produces and the chemical content of that saliva. Two of these were specifically mentioned: "Uppers" and "Downers." These drugs, used with prescription as diet pills or tranquilizers, *will* have harmful effects on your oral health. Ask your M.D. and your dentist to consider this aspect and advise you about diet-intake modification if, for some reason, you *must* use these medications.

If you are, by the way, a "speed freak," someone whose intake of amphetamines far exceeds common sense; either through addiction or the notion that this artificial "bracer" makes you more productive, you can expect *serious* dental problems. If you're in this category, you should get medical-dental counseling immediately.

That same advice would hold true for those whose intake of tranquilizers is either high or long term: Get to an M.D. or a dental doctor who knows what he's doing, and discuss this with him. Either of these drugs is an accelerator if you're driving down the road toward denture city.

Okay...so the "summary" advice is to avoid sweets for prolonged periods, or too often. If you can bring your dietary habits into a sensible, well-balanced intake, and if you are performing effective oral hygiene, you can all but forget about sugar as a major factor in odontosis.

You should know that ingesting any food which the mouth rapidly begins converting to sugar will almost instantly cause high acid production if there is odontosis in the mouth. More important, however, is the knowledge that while the increase in acid is enormous and instantaneous, it takes a long time for the production to taper off.

If you can find or take the time to brush your teeth and/or rinse you mouth after ingesting concentrated, highly refined sugar, you should.

(Oramedics doctors and patients are often seen driving from lunch back to their office...or to work, or whatever, while busily brushing their teeth. Why not...?)

While you are developing your own personal hygiene; before you've had your clinical tests and have the confidence that you've completely controlled odontosis in your own mouth, you'd be well advised to limit your use of foods with long sugar-retention-times. Some ground rules:

Don't eat hard candy, or any food with a lot of sugar in it that is consumed by slowly melting it in your mouth. The reason for this is, of course, obvious.

Do you use sugar in your coffee or tea? —Stop it! If you must have sweetener in it, use an artificial sweetener. Sure, there's been a lot of flack in the news lately about the "harm" these sweeteners might do to your health. Weigh that against the damage it will do to your health if you soak disease germs in raw sugar.

Do you chew gum? Shame on you! Sweetened chewing gum has one of the highest release-times on the list. This is totally unnecessary: There are chewing gums on the market that are sweetened without sugar. Some of them are sweetened with something called Xylitol...and *that* chemical is actually *beneficial* for your oral health.

For your guidance, we are going to give you a table showing the clearance times of various foods. This table will show the comparative times for each of these to "clear;" to reduce sugar-related acid production first to one-half of its immediate impact, and then to "safe" levels.

FOOD TYPE	½ Safe	Safe
Boiled Potatoes	2.5	9.6
Boiled Macaroni	2.9	12.2
Toffee	2.7	16.8
Chocolate Cream	2.9	16.1
Caramel Candy	3.2	18.8

FOOD TYPE (Cont.)	½ Safe	Safe
Milk Chocolate	3.6	12.2
Brown Rye Bread	3.8	18.9
White unsweetened bread	4.0	20.1
Wheat Biscuits	4.0	21.1
Wheat Bread, sweetened	4.4	21.4
White sweetened bread	5.9	25.7
Chewing Gum with sugar	7.4	42.2

(Time in minutes)
Source: *Journal of Preventive Dentistry*

Point of interest: If you average the clearance times above, by category, you'll find that the overall average for the starchy foods is the same as that for the outright candy: 16 to 19 minutes. Is that a mind-opener? It should be! Why? —Remember what your dentist preaches...avoid sweets? —How?!

If you have active dental disease, and you are still conscientious about your toothbrushing habits, you probably feel that you ought to get to a toothbrush an hour or so after eating a delicious chocolate sundae.

Go ahead, if it makes you feel better. We don't really want to spoil your good habits, or upset your peace of mind...but, let's face facts:

If you have odontosis, and you eat a chocolate sundae, and you don't brush your teeth and rinse your mouth sometime within about fifteen minutes after you've eaten it...

Forget it. You're too late. If you don't have odontosis you can safely brush when you get around to it, with no fear of decay.

At the bottom line of all this, we come back (again) to the necessity for decisions: There are only two ways that you, as an individual, can limit the damage of disease-caused acid upon your oral environment.

You can, as the dentist says, "avoid sweets" —making an all-out effort to deprive yourself of many foods, living a life that is one of constant self-supervision and nutritional awareness. This might help, depending on how well you do it; and how consistently.

The other way is to control the germs that actually produce the acid. Without them, raw sugar has no practical effect on your teeth.

When your saliva test and Navy Plaque Index results indicate "zero disease" in your mouth, go ahead and reward yourself with that delightful confection. If the rest of your system is in good shape, you don't have a thing to worry about.

Chapter Nine
The A.D.A. —Specialists in Symptoms

The American Dental Association is the power in organized dentistry —at least, it's the most visible expression of that power. Lurking behind the scenes there is the enormous power and authority of the dental colleges: A network of influence and vested billions of dollars which sorely needs scrutiny; a massive job waiting for some governmental organization dedicated to breaking up monopolies detrimental to the American public.

These schools doubtlessly "pull the strings" and manipulate or influence both the A.D.A. and the many state or federal governance agencies whose nominal function is to protect the consumer. A suppressed doctorial thesis explored this twilight zone of interlocking bureaucracies, agencies and influences: It makes fascinating reading for anyone who has the knowledge and experience to understand it. Unfortunately, there is only one "bootleg" copy of the thesis available; because the university involved made absolutely sure it would never be published.

Regardless of what ultimate power there is behind the scenes of American Dentistry, the professed and confessed "leader" is the American Dental Association. It is this organization that tells dentists what to do, when to do it, and how. It is this organization that has the lobbyists in state capitols and the federal government, "looking out for number one." The A.D.A. is the group that operates the "truth squad," highly-paid professionals who "help" and "advise" the media: Major newspapers, newswire services, radio and TV broadcasters.

The A.D.A. selects the men who will sit on the various state government boards and agencies; those agencies designed to protect the consumer from professionals who would do them harm; rip them off or in any manner exhibit "conduct unbecoming the profession."

Who do these agencies protect?

Do they really act to keep the "bad" doctors in line...or is their main function to protect, at all costs, the establishment? The answer to that question should be obvious to anyone who reads the newspapers with any regularity. Time and again, we discover that the regulatory boards and agencies of the state and federal governments are "packed" by people from within the vested interest ranks of the profession or trade which, supposedly, is "regulated."

There is no reason to suppose that dentistry is any different —and it isn't. In fact, there's pretty good evidence that most of the state agencies responsible for public dental health and welfare suffer from the same incestuous relationships as do other regulatory boards...only more so.

At the bottom line of all this...at least, at the visible bottom line...there is the American Dental Association and its state and local chapters. The A.D.A.'s spiderweb of influence emanates from national headquarters in Chicago, Illinois and reaches ultimately into every dental office in the nation. A dentist practising in Elephant Breath, Wyoming belongs to (automatically upon paying his dues) the Elephant Breath Dental Association, the Wyoming Dental Association, and the American Dental Association.

He can do anything, in his practice, that the A.D.A., W.D.A. and E.B.D.A. allow him to do...and nothing whatsoever these agencies consider a "no-no."

Does he have to belong to the dental associations? —Not at all. There's nothing in the licensing laws that mandate membership in the associations. He could decide to "go it alone" if he had the guts...but why should he? Membership is something that virtually every dentist does, if for no other reason than self-protection. If he *did not* belong to the organization, he would be watched night and day: One slip, one little "mistake" and he'd be up for charges of at least unprofessional conduct; and more than likely he'd be facing criminal sanctions: He'd lose his license to practice.

This is no more than basic, elementary human psychology carried to almost-paranoid extremes: If you are not "one of us," then you must be against us; if you're against us, we are going to "get" you sooner or later.

How does the A.D.A. "get" a dentist who is a maverick? First, there is the internal procedure: The kangaroo courts of the associations themselves, which results in excommunication from the brotherhood. If that doesn't do it...if the doctor hasn't learned his lesson from that...he next will find himself facing charges from the regulatory agencies of the state in which he practices.

Who runs these agencies? Textbook answer: The state government. Actuality: The American Dental Association. Do the lawyers who make up the state legislatures have the necessary knowledge and experience to write dental laws? —Of course not. They have to have expert help. Who is more than happy to supply the help, the advice and counsel? Right on: The A.D.A. Who sits on the boards who pass judgement on doctors "brought up on charges?" You got that right: Dentists sit on those boards.

Who selects the men who will sit on those boards? Depending on the method of the state, it will be an appointee of the governor, or someone selected by a legislative committee; or perhaps simply a function of a bureaucratic agency within the government. In any case, they must get a list of candidates from somewhere, in order to select the members of the regulatory board.

Where do you suppose they get that list?

Sure: From the A.D.A.

Thus, the profession of dentistry is "policed" by two agencies: There is the self-policing of the dental association, with the authority to sanction its own members; and there is the criminal power of the state.

Question: What word would you use to describe the relationship of a man cohabitating both openly and secretly with his sister?

What word would you use to describe a process which selects "policemen" to police a profession —from the ranks of that profession? —And, not only that, but which lets the profession write the laws and then administer the justice?

If that isn't incest, it will surely do until a better example comes along.

In a later chapter, we'll take a walk-through a case history —Dr. Nara's —and then let you judge for yourself how the A.D.A. administers "justice" and polices its ranks. For now, we wanted you to have this much background so that you could understand better why you will not find a preventive dentist in your home town...at least, not very easily.

We subtitled this chapter "The A.D.A. -Specialists in Symptoms" because we wanted to show you how the use of recognized dental specialties is yet another way the A.D.A. keeps dentists locked in to "business as usual," preventing the innovative or socially-conscious man from telling the public about his services.

There are recognized dental specialties: They are recognized by the A.D.A. and adopted by the several state legislatures as the "only" dental specialties in the profession. A dentist may advertise (discreetly, and only if his state allows it) when he is a practitioner in one of these specialties. He becomes a specialist by fulfilling the A.D.A. -established requirements as to special education, experience, etc. It would be stupid to tell you that there is no favoritism or politicking within the A.D.A. as to who gets to specialize and who doesn't —so we won't try to tell you that. There is, of course, some correlation between capability, education and experience and the license to specialize; but there is also a good deal of politics involved. This isn't necessarily only true of dentistry, and we are not trying to belabor the point. We just wanted to let you see still another way the A.D.A. uses pressure to make dentists conform.

There wouldn't be any chance that a maverick, an innovator could hope to get a specialty license. If a doctor isn't "party line" right down to his local association level, he might as well forget about ever being licensed in a specialty...even one of the recognized specialties.

The specialties recognized by the A.D.A. are these: There is the specialist in children's dentistry; and the specialist in orthodontics (braces, corrective dentistry). There is a specialist in oral surgery... although all dentists are Doctors of Dental Surgery (DDS), they are not all specialists in oral surgery.

There is the man specializing in "prosthetics" —he specializes in dentures, but what he actually does to and with his profession of dentistry is more akin to the world's oldest profession; the faintly-reminiscent sound of the word "prosthetics" will give you a clue.

The periodontist does pretty much what the name would lead you to suspect: He is principally concerned with periodontal problems —gum problems —and he is a dentist...so the name periodontist.

There is a recognized and therefore supposedly honorable specialty in extracting teeth: The A.D.A. super-licenses men to do the very last thing any socially responsible dentist would do.

But there is no specialty for preventive dentistry; nor is it likely that there will be in the forseeable future. If the A.D.A. recognizes the "handwriting on the wall" and tries to clean up its act in a hurry; if the pressure bought by private citizens and government agencies begins to "move" the A.D.A., then they will perhaps "license" specialty in preventive dentistry.

If they do, you may be sure they'll do it in such a way that only their favored sons get the specialty license...and there will be so many restrictions and limitations placed upon it that it will be longer be recognizable as preventive dentistry.

In short, there will not be a specialty in effective preventive dentistry as long as the A.D.A. is alive and well and able to react, knee-jerk fashion, to any threat to the continued billions of dollars of annual income garnered because of dental disease.

So, as far as you are concerned, there is no way to locate a specialist in preventive oral medicine. No dentist may advertise any differently that any other dentist unless he is a specialist: The only thing he may advertise then is what specialty he practices. Since there is no preventive medicine specialty recognized by the A.D.A. and its incest-relative state agencies, there will never be an advertisement that you can use to locate effective dental preventive medicine.

Dr. Nara's two-line advertisement in the Yellow Pages (in small type) said, "Specializing in Oramedics —For people with teeth who want to keep them." That advertisement cost him his membership in the local, state and national chapters of the A.D.A. and subsequently directly resulted in a twelve-month suspension of his license to practice in the state of Michigan.

Oddly enough, there was another "illegal" ad in those same Yellow Pages. Another dentist listed his practice as "General Dentistry." This is mentioned in passing only to further underline the paranoia of the A.D.A.: They didn't (or haven't yet) bring charges against that dentist: He's "one of theirs," a party-liner. What he did "wrong" is list a non-existent specialty: There is no such specialty as "General Dentistry," any more than there is a recognized specialty of "Oramedics." If a dentist is not a specialist, he automatically practices "general dentistry."

The point, of course, is that the ad for General Dentistry is wholly as illegal as the ad for Oramedics: Either is "holding himself out as a specialist in an unrecognized specialty."

One was ignored. The other lost his license for a year. The question is, of course, "why?" —And the answer is an entire book: "Money By The Mouthful."

For you to locate a dentist who wants to practice preventive oral medicine, you'll have to simply "shop around" for dental care the same way you would for an appliance or a used car. Why not? Who on earth said you had no right to look for the best deal in health care, if you can for machines?

Visit your dentist and tell him the things you've learned in this book. Ask him quesions about it. Ask if he will give you a lactobacillus saliva test...and if he feels it would tell him anything about the state of your oral health. Ask if he can administer a Navy Plaque Index Test...and if that's something he'd like to do before he gets carried away with his drills, knives and plastic junk.

Ask if he does bite-wing or full series X-rays before completing a diagnosis of disease damage. If he loftily informs you that bite-wings are standard for the profession; that almost all dentists rely on them...he's right —run like the dickens! He's a butcher.

If he wants to use a dental explorer on you (a sharp probe he uses to find soft spots or cavities in enamel), tell him "no, thanks!" and get out of there. (More about this in a later chapter about iatrogenic disease, appliances, and "hardware" that'll make you sick.)

Obviously, if he's more interested in "fixing" the symptom damage he finds in your mouth than he is in talking about the disease that caused the damage, you're wasting your time and money.

Don't simply ask the dentist if he practices preventive dentistry. The A.D.A.'s public relations mill grinds out this theme day after day: That all dentists are "prevention-minded." That is an unconscionable lie; they are not, they haven't been and they don't intend to be prevention-minded. They are disease-causing, not disease-curing; they make a living repairing symptomic damage and no amount of public relations heat and steam changes the truth.

So the question, "Do you believe in preventive dentistry" has no meaning. The dentist believes the A.D.A. —he'll say, "sure" —even as he reaches for his explorer to cause you unnecessary pain and discomfort; and to inoculate healthy teeth with disease germs.

You'll need to take the information you're learning in this book, and confront the dentist with some hard questions: If he is happy to answer them, if he seems pleased that you know about disease germs, about plaque and Strep. mutans and Lacto...if he gets interested in doing saliva cultures and NPI tests...you've probably located a dentist who can help you achieve and maintain freedom from dental disease.

Any dentist who shows distaste for these things and a preference for his machinery over talking about disease is one of the thousands and thousands who simply doesn't care whether you ever get free from disease or not...

Or, maybe, he's one of those who realizes that if the people of America ever learn the truth "en masse," he'll be out of business. Maybe he's one of the dentists who knows that when we're out of disease...he's out of an income.

Shop around. Most dentists, following the lead of the A.D.A., are Specialists in Symptoms. A few, following their brains and hearts, are specialists in prevention...but they don't tell you about it, because the A.D.A. won't let them.

They *can* talk to you about it in the privacy of their own dental offices...the A.D.A. hasn't got "bugs" there...and a good preventive-oriented dentist will be happy to do so.

Be prepared for some angry reactions: Many dentists will be upset at your approach; some will react against you all out of proportion to the words you use.

Some will try to ridicule you; to browbeat you with their "superior knowledge." They'll try to make you feel cowed by their authority as doctors.

Hang in there. You have every right to question a dentist thoroughly about what he intends to do, and how he intends to do it, before you even pay him a dime or establish one red cent indebtedness.

There's more than just your money at stake; there's your oral health and physical health: A very large and important part of your future depends on the capability and attitude of the next dentist who wants to reach into your mouth.

If enough people do this with enough dentists, we will all be helping to bring health to America and the dental profession into the twentieth century. The reward for being part of this may seem remote and impersonal; but it is valuable to our nation and our nation's children.

There is, however, an immediate and very personal reward for people who make dentists perform health services instead of symptom repairs: The reward, of course, is personal freedom from dental disease; freedom from future pain and expense and poor health. Isn't it worth it?

Chapter Ten

Psychology of Oral Health Awareness

Don't let the chapter title scare you off: We haven't gotten overly technical before now and we aren't going to in this chapter. Psychology isn't necessarily a technical subject, anyway...at least, not practical applied psychology.

You use it —and have it used on you —every day. Advertising is almost pure psychology: If you separated the genuine value information from the surrounding "sales pitch", advertising wouldn't have much left, would it?

Don't you use some psychology on your kids...on your spouse...on your boss or your subordinates...or, at least, don't you try to?

Oramedics believes in psychology. It is a major part of the approach used in Oramedics practices, and with very good reason: We are involved in behavior modification. We are trying to get people to change some of their habits.

What causes behavior? Simply: Isn't it the way we perceive reality; and how we react to what we think reality is? That's all there is to your personal approach to dental (oral) hygiene, isn't it? You perceive (or mis-perceive) reality as, "There's nothing anyone can do about bad teeth" —and you react to it: "What's the use of trying?"

At Oramedics we are dedicated to changing the perception of reality so that the way we "see" it is closer to the way it really "is." If you can grasp the dynamic significance of this one, single element of Oramedics principles you will have received full value from this book. Let's say it again (and again, if need be): We (you) are vitally involved in changing a *frame of reference* —the way we (you) perceive reality; so that the way you see it matches the truth.

That's why we got slightly involved in psychology. It's probably important that you understand *why* you have been able to wholly, completely believe a set of outmoded "truths" that were dangerous to your health.

We perceive reality essentially through *cognitive* processes; which means that there is some thinking involved. Compare the mind briefly to a computer: It is first programmed, then it is fed a series of data —then it is asked to deliver a statement, a summary, that is compatible with the programming and the facts given it.

A computer *cannot* arrive at information through *conative* processes: These are uniquely human characteristics and we know them by names such as "insight," "intuition" or "hunch". It is the *conative* aspect of human decision-making that renders us emotional; and emotions are something a machine cannot and does not have.

Thus our perception of reality is both rational and logical; resulting from programming (what we are told) and evidence (what we see), and it is at the same time emotional —colored or influenced by what we *want* to believe...or what we despair of believing.

What are some of the things we are "programmed" to believe about dental disease? Well, there's the classic: "Brush after meals, use floss, avoid sweets, and *see your dentist twice a year.*"

—In other words, the best we can do *still* results in the probability that we need "something done to our teeth" every six months.

Advertising? —"only one cavity," or "30% fewer cavities," or "can be of significant value" (that's a sweetheart, that one...it means, bluntly, that there was enough data so that it could be measured...not exactly overwhelming, is it?). Let's take a further look into advertising: Prime time TV, right? Your living room, the center of your household, right? You and the kids sitting there, being "programmed" (is brainwashed a better word?)...What you see most often in dental advertising is for *dentures*! You are flooded with misinformation about adhesives and cleansers and deodorants all of which are *primarily designed* to "sell" you on the benefits of denture products. These advertisements cost hundreds of thousands of dollars; you'd better believe they are psychologically "loaded" to hit you at every level of your cognitive and conative processes. Will they make a "believer" out of you? *They sure will!*

While the individual companies are vying with one another to get you to believe in their own product over the other guy's, what the sum total of their advertising is doing to you is programming you to accept the flat-out lie that dentures are inevitable and beneficial.

They *are not* inevitable...and they are extremely dangerous to your health. The problem is: *How* are you going to know that unless the misinformation is counteracted?

Remember: You perceive reality through (1) programming, through (2) thinking about information you're given, and (3) through insight, intuition, emotion.

You've been programmed all your life against any hope that dental disease can be avoided, so we can forget that aspect. For the second hope: Who would tell you the truth, so you can arrive at rational, logical decisions? —Would your dentist, or the A.D.A.? Here's a little something for you to think about: Every time you see or hear an advertisement which mentions the A.D.A. as "recognizing" the product's value, that means the A.D.A. has *endorsed* it. Analyze the next several denture-related advertisements and see how many of them have the A.D.A. stamp of approval...

Your final avenue of perception is your own insight, and the cards are stacked against this to an insurmountable degree. Your mom and dad had bad teeth. Your husband or wife has bad teeth. You have bad teeth...hey; your *dentist* has bad teeth! Surrounded by this sea of dental disease, your insight has no chance to make the quantum-leap through to the truth. Emotionally, you are geared more toward despair than hope; and this subconscious reverse-insight has a powerful effect on your rational thinking.

Your perception of "dental reality" —your frame of reference toward dental disease —has set you up like a clay pigeon: Your name has become "target" and guess who is sitting on the firing line? Two bad actors you've already met, earlier in this book: *Lactobacillus acidophilus and Streptococcus mutans.* What will they do to you? They'll destroy your dental health and damage your overall health.

Of course, you knew that all along, didn't you …even before you read this book?

What you *didn't* know was that these germs, and the odontosis they are responsible for, is totally, absolutely preventible…it *does not have to happen* …those denture product advertisements should be a waste of time and money; you ought to ignore them…or laugh at them!

This chapter on "psychology" is to help you feel fully grounded in your "new" frame of reference. It is going to be tested, the first time you talk to a dentist; or when your next-door neighbor, "the world's foremost authority," gets a can of beer under his belt.

You should understand, about yourself and your new perception, that it is presently based only on *inductive reason:* In other words, we've been throwing a lot of facts at you, facts, that, taken together, make a lot of sense. You've been able to reason; to tie things together with logic, and to modify your belief patterns accordingly. We have *not* been able to do anything about your pre-programmed beliefs; nor have you, as yet, had any empirical proof that we are telling the truth.

We've given you the basic tools with which you can employ both cognitive (thinking) and conative (insight) understanding, but we can't —in a book —give you the actual experience you will need before your perception becomes grounded in personally-experienced fact.

When someone challenges your new thinking, they will sooner or later ask you to prove it. As of now, you can't...you can give them this book to read; or you can cite some of the evidence we've offered...but you can't "prove it," at least not yet.

Be careful of this...because you are one of a relatively few people who have ever found all of this information in one place, between the two covers of a single book. No dentist has...unless he's read this same book. Your neighbor hasn't; your co-workers haven't. They will still view odontosis through the old frame of reference...and they will be just as "sure" of themselves as you once were, when you shared that frame of reference.

"They" are going to try to shake you. Your oral health hangs on your ability to resist both challenges to your new-found perception and the "tug" of the old, familiar way of thinking; a perception and set of values that is more comfortable than these new values simply because it is familiar; you're "used to it."

Before any of this book can personally benefit you, it must be the catalyst that causes you to *modify your behavior.* Just knowing about these things won't do you any good unless you do something about what you know. When we accept that behavior as the way we react to our perception of reality, then the value of this book is to *change reality* about your oral health...so you can *react differently* —by taking charge of your own dental destiny.

Only after you begin reacting in different ways to the new reality will you begin to accrue the personal, empirical proof that dental disease can be conquered; and not whether we can stamp it out worldwide...but only whether we can eliminate it in your own mouth.

When you talk to someone about these things today or tomorrow, they'll challenge you: "Prove it."

You won't be able to.

If you modify your behavior and begin to participate actively in controlling the factors of dental disease, and if you do it for a month to six weeks, it will then be a whole different story.

Then, when someone challenges you to "prove it," you can smile and say something like this: "Would you be willing to bet a hundred dollars in cold, hard cash that there is any active disease in my mouth?"

You see, when your own, personal Navy Plaque Index is down below or near level three, and when your saliva culture indicates no organized bacteria activity, *you will have conquered odontosis.*

Today, we want you to hang on tight to this thought: "I believe..."

Next month, we want you to be able to say it a bit differently: "I *know!*"

There is one other thought we should look at before we leave this chapter on psychology of oral health: What's in it for *me?* We are all motivated, at the bottom line, by personal loss or gain; by the twin goads of fear or reward, the attraction of the carrot or the threat of the stick.

Is freedom from odontosis worth changing the way we look at things? Is it worth modifying behavior so that we are actively participating in our own dental destiny?

If this book is telling the truth, what do you have to gain? If you don't do anything about your dental destiny, what have you got to lose? Why should you let this book affect your life at all?

Well, first of all, you don't have anything to lose when you come right down to it. If none of this makes sense, or if you do your best to modify your behavior and still nothing comes of it, you haven't lost anything. Your dental health is bad and getting worse right now anyway, isn't it? So what else is new?

What benefit could there be, if this book is telling it like it is and if you modify your behavior? —We could tell you about clean, pretty teeth as a benefit.

We might want to try to sell you on the idea of socially-acceptable breath. We should emphasize the pleasure of eating what you want to, when and where you want to. There are many, many "plus benefits" of good oral health. To summarize; to make this whole thought meaningful, let's just mention one factor:

You have nothing to lose if we're wrong. We'll "give" you an extra ten years on your life-span if we're right. Would you like that repeated? Okay: If we're right, and you modify your oral health behavior, you might very well live an additional ten years beyond what you otherwise would have. How's *that* for incentive?

Is that based on some sort of statistic? No, it isn't: It's a personal observation; but one we think most people can trust. Doctor Charles Mayo, founder of the famous Mayo Clinic in Rochester, Minnesota, observed that all other things being equal, denture wearers could look forward to the loss of about ten years from their lifetime.

Hopefully, this chapter has given you some insight into your own thought process, your own decision-making process. If so, it will have helped you begin to use this new-found knowledge to move from the perception stage to the behavioral stage... because it won't do you *any* good to "know" these things if you don't *use* them.

In short, we now hope and expect that you will:

1. *Discard your old programming,* your "frame of reference."
2. *Study and absorb* this new information, and think about it long and carefully; so that it becomes your new "frame of reference."
3. Begin *changing your behavior* so that you can, as soon as possible, begin to build up positive experiences to shore up your knowledge.

You haven't anything to lose, really....

And there's a whole lot to gain. You know that —why not put it to work for yourself? —For your family?

Chapter Eleven
The Hardware Business

Everybody knows that the dentist is in the hardware business. Did you ever play word-association games? Let's try it. Dentist: Fillings.

Try again. Dentist: Drill.

One more time. Dentist: Braces.

See how the game is played? I say "dentist," and you respond with a word that's going to (a) hurt, (b) cost a bundle, or (c) both.

As a matter of fact, your friendly dentist couldn't make it without all that hardware. It's his ticket to the country club, the new car and the nice home on the "right" side of town. Think about it: How would your dentist make his living if he didn't sell all that hardware...and charge an arm and a leg for it? *What has he to offer* once you take the hardware away from him?

Until now, you've only thought about that —if at all —in terms of what it means to you, personally. Now we want you to realize that you're talking about a multibillion dollar annual industry: The dental hardware business. Take your hometown dentist...multiply times however many dentists there are in this country ...and you begin to realize the magnitude of what we're talking about.

If you had no other reason to understand why Oramedics gets such fierce resistance from organized dentistry, this one aspect alone should tell you something.

Whether it's organized crime, or organized medicine, or organized dentistry...*organized* anything with an entrenched system that pumps billions of dollars a year —without sending people to jail —is going to fight like a tiger when the system is threatened.

Oramedics threatens the hardware game in dentistry as no other aspect of the profession is threatened. We have found the way to eliminate dental disease: That alone kills a huge percentage of the drill-and-fill hardware sales. It does more, though: It destroys the super-lucrative retail sales of dentures and all the denture-related goodies you can find advertised right in your living room almost any evening on prime-time TV.

Even if it stopped there, Oramedics would be something organized hardware sales money would be fighting. It doesn't stop there, however.

Oramedics doctors are not orthodontists...except in the sense that any general dental practitioner is familiar with orthodontics; but not a specialist in the field. As general practitioners with a difference, Oramedics doctors know enough about misaligned or deformed teeth to know the causes...and the correction.

That, however, is where the Oramedics doctor and the general, run-of-the-mill dentist —and the orthodontists —have their disagreement.

Anyone who has ever had a child with a bite-pattern problem, corrected by orthodontic appliances, will know how terribly expensive it is. Those braces, and the fees for fitting them, can put mom and dad in the poorhouse. It would be bad enough if it was a one-shot deal; but it isn't...is it? The teeth and the kid keep growing, and every six months it's a re-vamp in there, all that jungle of stainless steel and chrome is replaced with another contraption and —bring money, right?

When you take your child to the dentist (every six months, like a good momma, right?) he checks for "normal" growth, in between drilling and filling. Suppose he finds something not where it should be. What does he do about it?

He does *nothing* about it, that's what he does.

Instead, he tells you with a sad shake of his head, "there's a problem with the bite...I think you should take this child to an orthodontist, a specialist..."

What do you do, then? Of course...the dentist

gave you advice; you paid through the nose for it...so what *would* you do? You'd go see the orthodontist, right?

This guy takes a look, after you've already told him that the general practitioner found trouble developing, and he says, "There's a problem developing, there. It's too early, now; bring the child back in about six or eight months and we'll see what we have to do about it."

Now...did the specialist *do* anything? No, he sure didn't. He looked in the mouth, thought about what you told him, and agreed with the G.P. What is that? ...that's nothing, right?

Did he charge for this "service?" Of course he did!

Now —you still don't have anything going for you except the advice of doctors, first the G.P. and then the specialist. They've both scared you with their talk about a developing problem, but neither of them has done anything. What are they waiting for?

They're waiting for the problem to get really bad...so bad that your child's health begins to suffer, and the deformation of the teeth is beginning, maybe, to have a cosmetic effect that is tearing that adolescent ego to bits. Once the damage gets bad enough, then —and only then —will the "doctors" do anything. And what the doctor will do is to hang wires and hooks and maybe pegs in the mouth, hoping to put enough tension on the teeth that they'll grow into their proper place.

If you've been through this, you may be thinking, "Tell me something I *don't* know!"

All right, how's this: The whole thing was probably preventible; and if there was correction needed, it could have been done, earlier, for so little money that it would seem almost free compared to the fees for orthodontic devices.

An Oramedics doctor would have conducted, routinely, something called a "mixed dentition analysis." This isn't something your dentist never heard about; it's just something that he doesn't pay much attention to, if he's like most dentists.

There's a method of classifying tooth evolution or development; there are methods of finding out whether the jaw is "normal" or "prognathic" (jutting), or "retruded" (receding). Other information is also readily available to the dentist when he (carefully) examines a child's teeth and (carefully) conducts an overall oral evaluation.

Perhaps the wisdom teeth are crowding other teeth as they push their way into place. Maybe there are other teeth which are crooked...for any number of reasons. The point is that this doesn't happen overnight, or even in a rapid period of time. It can't! And if it's caught early, and something is done about it, it can be fairly easily corrected.

The thing that shouldn't happen is to see the problem developing, to send the child to an "expert" who in turn actually advises you to wait until the damage is done before he does something about it.

By the time the G.P. and the orthodontist have finished with you, they've got you right where they want you: Scared, confused, and "minding" them when they give you instructions.

They even give you time to go somewhere and dig up the money before you have to make a payment for the expertise and binding wire that will end up in your kid's mouth.

Had the problem been addressed early enough, the dentist would have been able to take care of natural growth and development in such a way as to make eventual bracing and appliances unnecessary. For one example: Often use of an inexpensive rubber or plastic mouthpiece, held in the mouth simply by biting on it, can correct a misalignment problem that could only be corrected with hard bracing if it developed fully.

For many years, patients in one Oramedics practice have been able to get a complete analysis of their child's natural growth and development for less than twenty five dollars. Many youthful patients were helped at the critical time by corrective extraction of unnecessary teeth, or by inexpensive appliances, or other means.

Parents of these children saved thousands of dollars over the years. That, in itself, is important; but there's perhaps even a more important consideration: Young, growing children are at their most emotionally-vulnerable point during the same time that teeth are growing into their final place. For those with mis-alignment; with crooked teeth or jutting (or receding) jaws, the world is a cruel place filled with jokes and jibes about the teeth. It is a world of missed dates, of melancholy: It can be a time when a lifetime "complex" is formed.

Even for those children fortunate enough to be in a family able to afford orthodontic care, there is this ego problem. Picture a pretty girl; young, full of hope...bashful, perhaps a bit shy...a girl with a beautiful smile when she is moved to smile.

Now...picture the same girl with braces, that hideous row of metal pickets across the teeth. Now she's stopped smiling, fearful that all she has to do to lose everything in her society is to open her mouth.

The psychological impact of such unnecessary hardware sales, especially on the young, is something we will never be able to measure as we can measure the hundreds of thousands of dollars poured into the hardware game each year. But...it is there, and it is real. And, if the profession would get honest about it and stay honest about it, most of it is wholly un-necessary.

There is one other bad side-effect of such hard-ware. By now you are really familiar with the cause of dental disease: Germs, which find safe harbors in which to build their colonies. Can you think of a better place than to get behind all that wire and harnessing?

Think of how hard it is to get the teeth really clean in those areas...

All of this could be prevented, usually, if the general practitioner would *pay attention* to what he sees inside the mouth of a six to eight year old child. During this critical time, between baby teeth and permanent adult teeth, the problems that can be prevented have their onset.

A predictive graph can be made by the dentist, which will tell him with great accuracy how the teeth are likely to develop. In other words: When a child is between the age of six and nine, the general practitioner should be able to *predict* whatever orthodontic problems are likely to develop.

As an example, the crowding caused by wisdom teeth coming in might be forcing other teeth into incorrect alignment. Removal of the offending (and unnecessary) teeth would remove the pressure. Natural growth and development takes over, then...very much similar to the way trees will grow toward their lifegiving sunshine; will send roots toward their water supply. Proper growth is *natural*: In the example above, the horseshoe-shaped encirclement of muscle... the cheeks, the tongue...would exert an unceasing, gentle and wholly natural pressure, slowly but surely forcing the growing teeth into their natural positions.

Even if the situation is already so severe that unaided nature cannot correct it, the general practitioner can help with inexpensive and impermanent appliances.

All of these things can be done, and done well, by a competent general practitioner. There is no genuine reason...we think there is no excuse...to ignore these problems as they develop, only to refer the young patient to a specialist when it's too late for mother nature to do anything about it "with a little help from her friends."

The other part of "the hardware game" that people are most familiar with is the denture racket.

There is no other name for it: It is a racket, pure and simple; one which costs America literally millions of dollars a year in unnecessary expense.

The dentist buys a set of dentures...upper and lower...for not to exceed fifty dollars; usually less. These he "fits" into your mouth. The charge: Anywhere from $250 to —you name it. The sky is the limit; go for all the traffic will bear. Why not? There is no law against what the dentist charges or does (or doesn't do) with respect to dentures. In fact, the A.D.A. is so pleased with this side of the business, they've actually set up a specialty for it.

It's sort of a reward system: When a dentist has been a good drill-and-fill man for years, when he's played the A.D.A. game by the rules and been a "good boy," there comes a time when he's getting on in years and needs a safe, sure and —above all —easy way to rake in the income to which he's become accustomed.

What better way than to specialize in dentures? If you could average two hundred dollars or more *per patient* —clear profit —what would *you* do? That, of course, is provided your conscience had become so hardened and blistered over the years of general practice that it didn't bother you to sentence each and every one of your patients to an average 10 years deducted from their natural life span.

—And, of course, provided it didn't prick your sense of decency to charge a margin of profit above and beyond anything in the plumber's wildest dreams...

And, finally...it would have to bother you not one little bit that you first have to yank out every tooth in your patient's mouth...the good, the bad and the indifferent...before you can slap in that pile of junk plastic that costs less than fifty bucks wholesale...

The A.D.A. and your local dentist will tell you that it takes a great deal of skill to properly "fit" the dentures; that's why, they'll say, it requires the learned judgment and steady hand of a doctor.

Bullroar! The doctor is in and out of the room while the dentures are being "fitted," but he doesn't have to be: That's window dressing. That lady in the green smock that had you "bite down" on some gunk... *she's* the one who "fitted" your dentures. All that was required was to take an impression to send off to the factory where the false teeth are made. The dentist gets them back, U.P.S., and sets up an appointment for you to come in to be cared for. His skill, essentially, is in knowing how to open the package without your seeing it...and, if he has a busy denture practice, perhaps in keeping track to be sure that Mrs. Jones' teeth don't end up in Mrs. Farley's mouth...

There's an entire town in the Carolinas with a major industry in "fitting" cheap dentures. The co-author made a trip there, once, to get some first-hand knowledge about how they operate.

The lady at the front desk made an appointment for the next day, and answered questions:

"Are you sure the doctor will be able to remove all my teeth tomorrow morning?"

"Yes, sir," she answered. No problem! She didn't even ask how many teeth I had, and there are only four missing...only two that would have been good to save, had I known about Oramedics years ago.

Next question: "How long will it take, after the extractions, before I get my false teeth?"

Answer: "Oh, you get them the same day...it will be all finished before noon..."

How much? Well, the entire thing would cost less than $200.00; extractions, false teeth...the works. Is it any wonder that people drive here from almost all over the country when it's "finally time" for false teeth? They can still save money, even when you consider the expense of traveling...

This office was owned and operated by a doctor of dental surgery. Think about the implications: A man who has a license which should be trusted is running a money mill with one single purpose: To yank teeth and sell dentures. Carried to this extreme, it's fairly easy to spot the cupidity and gross money-hunger that motivates these people. We can easily see how "wrong" it is to simply, on demand, pull all the healthy teeth in a man or woman's mouth and put dentures into place.

But...what's the difference between the money mill, which is at least honest enough to deliver precisely what it advertises...and your local general practitioner, with his pious statements about prevention and dental care, etc., etc?

Any dentist who willingly seeks denture business, no matter how much he'd like to hide it, is doing the same thing as these denture mills: He has found some way to ignore all the truth about dental disease he ever knew; he has learned how to conceal any pride or skill or professionalism he ever had...in order to make money —at your expense.

In one of its publications, the A.D.A. once made a grave pronouncement: "No dentist will extract a tooth unnecessarily, if he is given the option."

In other words, no dentist will do what he shouldn't do...unless the patient insists, or the insurance company won't pay for other services...or unless the dentist is "forced" into it by pressure from the kid's parents...

Can you see an M.D. in this position?

"Doctor, I don't care if you *can* save that hand: I'm sick and tired of this arthritis in my fingers and I want the arm amputated."

...no doctor would cut off an arm unnecessarily, if he is given the option...?

No *doctor would let anybody* —anybody —tell him what to do; neither the patient, or the insurance company, or anyone else. The *doctor* makes a decision based on his own knowledge and skill, prescribes a treatment, and insists upon its being carried out. If the patient doesn't want to do what the doctor says, he can just darn well find another doctor.

No medical dentist would let anybody talk him into loading the mouth with unnecessary hardware, either. If a patient has a tooth that bothers him, the *doctor* finds out why, and does something about it. And, he does more than care for one sick tooth. He realizes that the tooth is sick because the mouth is diseased...and he sets out to correct the medical situation that *caused* the problem.

The ordinary, run of the mill dentist never bothers to find out what the oral condition is. He doesn't care! A patient comes into his office, the dentist checks him over enough to find some "work" to do...and he does it.

Maybe he yanks out a tooth...especially if the tooth has had a history of aching, and the patient insists. The co-author lost one of his most important teeth in just that way: One day he got tired of the tooth "flaring up" from time to time and, with his jaw throbbing in pain, walked up two flights of stairs to a tacky office and told the dentist to "yank this damn tooth!"

He did. "Ten dollars, please."

Did he take X-rays? Of course not. Did he do anything to make sure the extraction wouldn't kill me —through bleeding, or infection, or what have you... weak heart, any number of possibilities? Of course not.

Did he offer to inform me that the reason my tooth ached was because there was a *disease* in my mouth? You know he didn't...how many dentists would?

There was another time, several years later, when the co-author tried the same thing, again; only this time, the dentist was named R. O. Nara.

And this time, the script was vastly different. "This tooth right here aches...let's pull it."

"Sure it aches...it's infected, there's pressure on that nerve. Just sit tight; we'll be right with you."

...then what happened? Well, the next thing was a nurse who came in and took X-rays; and not just bite-wings, either, but a full series of side and angle shots.

Then someone else came in and examined my mouth, carefully, and asked questions. I realized that I was giving my medical history! Wow...what *is* this?

Finally, Dr. Nara came back into the room, with a small bottle in one hand and a hypodermic syringe in the other. Now, I thought, we'd get down to business. I opened my mouth so he could "numb the nerve" with the hypo...

...And was startled, to say the least, when the assistant swabbed my shoulder with an alcohol swab. "What's that for?"

"You're going to get a shot, Cowboy," was Dr. Bob's reply.

"In the *arm?*"

"Where would you like it?" He asked, smiling. "It's an antibiotic; we can give it to you anywhere there's muscle —the arm's just the most convenient."

To make a long story short: The antibiotic was to kill off the infection (makes sense, doesn't it?) and the small bottle was a pain pill...because, after all, I'd come there to get rid of pain.

"I thought you were going to pull that tooth," I said.

"No way," the doctor said, "The tooth isn't too far gone...it's pretty bad, but it can be saved. Do you have *any idea* how important that tooth is to your health...?"

And that began my exposure to Oramedics, to a world where doctors tell patients, and not vice versa.

Suppose I'd gone to a conventional dentist; and suppose the tooth wasn't so bad that it could become badly infected. During the routine examination, the dentist would have found "a cavity" in the tooth.

Without further ado, he'd have reached for his drill and reamed out the cavity. He not only would have removed all of the diseased enamel, dentin and pulp or whatever...he'd have cut away a generous portion of healthy enamel.

In this, he'd have been doing what he was taught in dental school: It's called "extension for prevention" and it means that they make the hole larger than necessary. We won't go into the technical aspects of this; but there are far more compelling reasons *not* to do this than there are good reasons *for* it. In sum: Extension for prevention does not "prevent" dental disease. Only medical/hygiene care does that. The mechanical "prevention" simply replaces healthy enamel with amalgam (hardware again!). This weakens the tooth and, for various reasons, sets up a zone where active disease is likely to strike again later on. This kind of disease symptom, when it recurs, deserves the title "iatrogenic" —because there is no other way to say it than that the *doctor* caused it.

No mention of hardware is complete without talking about the dental explorer. This instrument is a torture device, of stainless steel and/or chrome, with a sharp point. It is a heavy-duty icepick, if you need a descriptive analogy.

With it, the dentist pokes and prys at your teeth, trying to locate "bad spots" in the enamel. It will leave your gums bleeding, it will cause you exquisite pain if the dentist manages to poke it into an active cavity.

If you jump, involuntarily, and let out a yip, the dentist will invariably ram it right back into the same hole...more or less to verify that, yes, indeed, you got a reaction that time, doc!

As he merrily moves from place to place in your mouth with this archaic device, scratching and gouging he is carrying live, active odontosis germs from infected areas to healthy areas. Should he successfully locate a cavity with this device, he will "fix" it with his drill and metal...sure...but what about the "clean" areas you came in there with? You may be sure that you will have another cavity when you return in six months, because the doctor infected a healthy area in your mouth, a place where you don't normally "catch" with your toothbrushing.

The dentist can do nothing with the explorer that he couldn't do at least as well...and probably better ...with a warm-air syringe and a mirror. There is not one legitimate reason to touch the teeth with a sharp instrument for the sake of examination...not one.

You can sum up your understanding of dental hardware with a fairly accurate generalization: It probably isn't necessary, you probably would have been far, far better off without it; if it *is* necessary, it's because of neglect in prior visits.

You may also fairly conclude that dental hardware is incredibly expensive; and you should by now realize that no matter how good hardware may be, the natural teeth are many, many times better...

You should also be aware that the hardware business is a lucrative business, so much so that there will continue to be an amazing amount of pressure "from the top" of organized dentistry to keep prevention from taking away "all the fun" of making money with substitutes for natural health...

As long as the industry is able to rake in the gross profits of billions annually by supplying hardware, there is no reason to expect the industry (profession) to voluntarily clean up its own act.

This profit comes from reacting with too little, too late, and in the wrong way, to the symptoms of disease. The profit comes from counter-acting symptoms while the disease goes on its merry way, uncontested and unrestricted.

As long as this disease continues to provide this kind of windfall profits in the hardware game, there will be no hope that the public can expect a fair shake.

The profession isn't about to give up a good thing.

The manufacturers, the public relations men, the advertising agencies...everyone with a finger in the multibillion dollar pie...of course, none of these will lift a finger to help you. Why should they cut off their own money source?

The government...? The government doesn't have anything to do with it...at least, not the federal government. The states, each of them, set up the laws governing dentistry. Those state laws are the *last* place you could look for help; they are written by dentists, and for dentists.

As it stands, today, the only protection you have from being a victim of the hardware racket is to be forewarned; to take the time and trouble to learn about it...

...and to make sure that there is no dental disease in *your* mouth, or in your family. That's the one certain way to avoid being fleeced by your dental "hardware dealer."

Chapter Twelve
A Question of Ethics

Why did the dental profession revoke Dr. Nara's membership in the A.D.A.? Why did the state of Michigan suspend his license?

They charged him with unethical conduct: He advertised an "unrecognized specialty" (Oramedics) and offered to save teeth.

That was his crime, and, according to the current laws of the states and the profession, that's unethical.

The National Health Federation's "Bulletin" featured the Nara story in a recent issue, and shortly after that publication was distributed, a letter arrived at the Oramedics office:

"Dear Dr. Nara:

I saw the National Health Federation Bulletin for July and August. I am stunned by the article on the cover relating to your loss of license. I do not live in Michigan but if I can sign a petition to support you please allow me.

"My son Dale H----- was your patient in 1966. Thanks to your preventive care he has a beautiful set of teeth today. When I moved to Illinois and tried to continue preventive dentistry I was unable to locate a dentist like yourself. Until I read the Bulletin yesterday I guess I didn't understand your program and just how important it is. You set this family on the road to good mouth care and we are very grateful to you.

"I will buy a copy of your book 'What Makes Johnny Run' for a better understanding of you and your profession.

"I support you and Oramedics for freedom of choice."

—A question of ethics? Let's ask another question, then, if we are concerned with ethics: Why was this lady unable to locate a preventive dentist when she was forced to move away from Dr.Nara's practice?

She wanted better dental health care for herself and her family; she sought it, she would have gladly

119

availed herself of such services. She was "unable to locate" the kind of dentist she preferred, because even if there had been that sort of dentists available, they cannot advertise their specialty" —it's unethical to be a preventive dentist.

—is *that* ethical?

Writing in a newsletter for the profession, Dr. Nara discusses this "specialty ache" with the following observation:

"After we have examined the psyche of dentists themselves, let's take a look at how we have structured the profession. We have two main categories: General Practitioners and Specialists. The general practitioners are all-around guys who do it all except some tough stuff they send to the specialists.

"Specialists: Those who keep learning more and more about less and less until they know everything about nothing.

"General Practitioners: Those who keep learning less and less about more and more until they know nothing about everything.

"Of our dental specialists we have quite a variety. We can start with the "Three R's" —Reamers (endodontists), Removers (Oral Surgeons) and Replacers (Prosthodontists). Then we have Pushers (Orthodontists) and Gum Cutters (Periodontists) and Pedodontists. The last is like a general practitioner only he does it on small people.

"Some specialists may take contest with my bit of humor here but my main point is to emphasize that all of these people *specialize* in super-sick teeth. The reason for the specialty in the first place is to deal with teeth that are so sick the G.P. won't touch them!

"*Why* don't we have a specialist who is a tooth saver, one whose special training requires that he know all about oral ecology, behavior modification, and health education? In the medical world there are about 15,000 doctors who have a specialty in preventive medicine. *Why* has this been left out of dentistry?"

When we discuss this whole thing as "a question of ethics," it seems that the dental profession has one very large question to answer before it can spout about ethics. The question is, "*why* doesn't the A.D.A. establish a specialty branch of dentistry which concerns itself with disease *prevention?*"

If the A.D.A. were to answer that question...if it could...the answer would probably be that "all dentists are qualified to practice prevention, and most do..."

The facts are that some nine out of ten Americans have disease in their mouths. If most dentists practice prevention, it doesn't show...anywhere.

The real answer lies in the proven fact that there is simply a whole lot of money to be had in concentrating on the symptoms...and a whole lot more in becoming a "specialist" allowing you to concentrate on even more advanced symptoms in even sicker mouths.

At the bottom line, it comes down to this: The A.D.A. and conventional dentists cannot exist without ongoing dental disease. If anyone ever successfully comes up with a preventive program, and manages to get it across to the American public in spite of organized dentistry's resistance, then dentists and dentistry as we know them today are a thing of the past. That goes double for specialists.

It's a matter of priorities, isn't it? Which is more important: Your health, or the dentist's income? The A.D.A. has decided that dental income is more important than dental health. They've proven themselves eminently qualified to pass judgment on money matters. When it's a question of professional income, conventional dentists have found all the answers.

When it's a question of ethics, any pronouncement by a member of organized conventional dentistry today would be obscene.

We can think of no more glaring hypocracy than for a man to render a trusting patient even sicker, so that he can make more money; and than turn around and make pious judgments against another dentist who simply wants to make his patients well...and to hell with the money!

There *is* a question of ethics involved, and it must be answered. We simply do not believe that members of conventional practices have any right, any longer, to answer the question.

We are asking it in the courts, today.

More importantly, however, we are asking *you;* right now, as an individual, to make a judgment.

We are considering what is, and what is not, the ethical way for a dentist to view oral health and its treatment.

You know what your dentist has done in the past.

You've read, now, enough to know what an "oramedics specialist" would do if you were *his* patient.

It isn't even so much a question of what he *does;* it is a question of whether he has the right to advertise it; to tell people what he would like to do.

The A.D.A. and many state laws say that it isn't a matter of fact; it's a question of ethics.

Well, we think it is, too...and we'd like you to decide the question.

A registered nurse in Wisconsin answered, for herself, this way:

'The ironic thing is that Michigan has a mandatory fluoridation law that is supposed to reduce tooth decay by an alleged 65%, and here is a dentist in Michigan who reduces it by 100% and he is expelled from the state dental society and loses his license to practice his profession. All because he dares to use a successful treatment not generally accepted by the establishment. This makes sense?

'I am glad Bob (Nara) is getting so much publicity —these narrow-minded societies need to be exposed.'

Do they...? These "narrow-minded societies" will never be exposed so long as *they* are the final arbiter of what is, and what is not, ethical.

The American public will have to make that decision...and, ultimately, we have faith that they will.

Chapter Thirteen
What Can I Do?

Until dentistry comes of age, the average citizen will have no hope of conquering dental disease (odontosis). If dentistry today held out any hope, how could the statistics on the prevalence of the disease be so gloomy? The prediction is for more of the same, no matter how much the "spokesmen" for organized dentistry talk about prevention, about fluoridation, about huge advances in the profession.

Until *most* dentists *practice* prevention, you'll just have to face the fact that prevention-oriented dentists are few and far between. If organized dentistry really meant it when they claim to be prevention-minded...why is it illegal, unethical and absolutely verboten to advertise that any one given dental practice is a preventive medical dental practice?

If you are within driving distance of an Oramedics practitioner, it would pay you to make the trip. One woman commuted from Chicago, Illinois to Houghton, Michigan for the specific purpose of saving her dental health. She was at that time a fairly highly placed executive with Playboy International, and so perhaps could afford the expense of the trip. She is convinced, of course, that she actually saved a great deal of money by not paying for remedial dentistry...and quite probably, she's right.

A number of Oramedics services are available through the mail; any reader who would like more (free) information about these services is welcome to write or telephone. The address is: Oramedics International, 200 East Montezuma Avenue, Houghton, Michigan 49931. Telephone: (906) 482-1419. A post card to that address will bring a response, including the nearest Oramedics practitioner (if any within reasonable distance), and other information about oral health and odontosis prevention.

In the meantime, there *are* some things you can

do. You probably won't be surprised to discover that the first thing is *not* to "see your dentist." You will have to see a dentist eventually, but not right away.

First, last and always: The name of the game is *keep it clean.* Nature cleanses and rejuvenates the whole body everyday, given half a chance. Our American diet and health habits are atrocious, and some of your habits will have to be changed. Make yourself a commitment, right now, or maybe you'd be better off simply forgetting this whole subject: You will have to keep after yourself until you've developed some new *habits.*

We don't mean that you have to become a slave to your toothbrush; we aren't talking about anything difficult to do. What we *are* talking about is habit, and it might be a good idea to define that a little bit.

A habit is something you do...well, habitually; right? In other words, you'd do it more often than not; usually without thinking about it very much. A habit becomes something that automatically finds a time-slot in your day, and other things must more or less work around that time.

If you have a habit, for instance, of starting your day with a cup of coffee and the morning paper, you always seem to find or make time for that small part of your day.

Things that are not a routine habit, on the other hand, can be put aside more easily. Example: Should I do my homework, or watch that movie on TV? —which would win that argument?

If you're already conscious of your dental hygiene, you are probably already investing about enough time daily to do the job: All we'll want you to do is restructure that time a little bit. If you are *not* hygiene conscious, maybe you'll have to do a little bit of thinking and planning about this.

However it works out for you, the important thing is this: You *must* create a psychology which provides the incentive to *do it,* and do it as a matter of routine habit. If you do, then the rare times when you miss because of some pressing, unusual circumstance will not harm you all that much. As we said earlier: You shouldn't be a slave to dental disease; you don't have to be a slave to dental hygiene. Remember the Oramedics motto: Oramedics is *freedom*...from dental disease.

Supplies: You'll need a good toothbrush. Don't buy a cheapie; it's not a daily or even a weekly (or monthly) investment. Get one for each member of the family. If your oral hygiene is presently not good, you'd be better off with a soft-bristle brush. For middle of the road cases, a medium-bristle is all right. The kind of brush that is shaped and angled to help you reach the tight spots is a good investment.

You'll need some dental tape, also. Look for tape (ribbon), not floss; and preferably a waxed tape. If your druggist doesn't stock it, pester him until he does.

Tooth powder is the next item. Earlier we discussed the relative merits of the various commercial preparations; you needn't be concerned with which is better. Any name brand powder will do the job better and less expensively than pastes.

Several companies are now marketing their brand of home-care tooth polishing machines. These are wand-shaped devices, battery-powered, with a number of interchangeable heads so that each family member can have his own color coded polisher.

This instrument will be advertised with words something like this: "Now you can do, at home, the same thing a dental assistant does when you have your teeth cleaned at the dentist's office..."

They're almost right. The device has a small electric motor that drives a little rubber cup at the tip of the wand. This thing, with commercially-available powders, will shine your teeth. It *doesn't* remove scale, tartar and calculus where it won't reach; and it isn't really a true substitute for a trained hygienist

126

...but it is good. If you can afford one, it's well worth it for the cosmetic improvement it will make in your appearance. Properly used (instructions come with the machines) it can also contribute to your overall oral hygiene; and anything that contributes to disease prevention is a good idea.

Irrigation devices are also available. One of the better known is the Water Pik (trade mark registered); which you may have seen advertised. This is not the only one available, but it is mentioned specifically to help you understand what an "irrigation device" is.

These things will squirt pressurized water pulses in a thin stream. If you are at all familiar with hydraulic mining principles, you can get an idea of how they do the job. This stream of water *can* reach where you *can't* reach with your brush. Here again, the irrigation device has a goodly amount of merit and is something for your consideration.

We also mentioned disclosing tablets in an earlier chapter, if you recall. To refresh your memory: These are food dye in tablet form, which you chew after brushing and taping your teeth. If there is any plaque in the mouth that you missed with your cleaning regimen, the tablets will dye the plaque. Clean areas are *not* colored, and so the "missed" areas stand out. A touch-up with the brush/tape will remove the offending plaque and the dye at the same time.

Disclosing tablets are great for teaching kids to take proper care of their teeth; but don't think of them as something for children only. Use them yourself; at least until you are very comfortable that you have become a "pro" at cleaning your teeth without this telltale signal of "whoops, you missed a spot."

Select a time of day most convenient for your new habit. The best time is at the end of the day, after supper and before bedtime. The time you select is not as important as whether you'll stick to it; so make it as easy on yourself as you can. One thing: Make sure you do this *after* your late, late snack. The obvious objective is to go to bed with a totally clean mouth; with the germs in a disorganized state (panic!), and with no bonanza of food and sugar for them to work on while you sleep.

You'll recall the contribution made by saliva to your overall oral health: During your sleep, the production of saliva is reduced. Many of us are "mouth-breathers" when sleeping, which further reduces the ability of saliva to flush the mouth, and to bathe the teeth with healing and restoring chemicals.

You'll swallow less often, in your sleep. Your saliva rate is lowered. Your mouth is dryer than normal; even more if you are a mouth-breather. By now you know about the mechanics of odontosis germs: Can you think of a better time for them to do their dirty work? That's why you *must* make an effort to avoid putting anything else in your mouth after your cleaning efforts and before going to bed.

You may like to use a mouthrinse, and it won't hurt you if you do. Anything you can buy without a prescription will be of dubious value in the war on disease, but if the use of a rinse makes you feel more like performing your hygiene, go right ahead.

If you'd like to mix a little baking soda and household (table) salt in with some tap water, you'll have a pretty good mouthrinse that won't cost you anything ...and it *will* help (a little bit) in the war on disease. Why? —Well, the process of odontosis involves acid, doesn't it? What's the opposite of acid? —Soda, right? To be more precise; alkalines are the opposites of acids...but soda doesn't get along with acid, either. Use it, as with any non-prescription rinse, if it makes you feel good.

How about fluorides...?

First of all: You can't get fluorides without a prescription unless the percentage of fluoride is extremely low. Such fluorides include public water fluoridation; toothpastes, rinses and other items you can purchase over-the-counter.

Will these help? Undisputedly, they *help*. If we can trust the statistics, they help quite a bit; meaning that the results can be scientifically measured. Again: Oramedics is in favor of *anything* that helps reduce the incidence of odontosis in America. Whether that ought to include involuntary fluoridation of public water supplies is not a medical question, it's a social-ethics question, and one Oramedics prefers not to discuss. Fluoride preparations *are* available for those who want them; perhaps we ought to question whether involuntary (forced) fluoridation is all that necessary...

However much they help, the non-prescription fluorides don't help *enough*. The danger is that parents using such preparations and providing them for children may be lulled into a false sense of security. Let's clear the air, once and for all. *Nobody* offers a non-prescription fluoride that will *prevent* odontosis. All such preparations are advertised (heavily) as "helping to reduce" dental decay (disease). They do what they claim; they do *not* do what the ad agencies would like you to believe.

If you are satisfied with reducing the damage of a disease that can be prevented absolutely, then you can depend upon commercially-available fluoride products to give you what you want. If, having come this far in this book, you are satisfied with half-measures, then either we have failed or you simply don't care about your own health.

Fluoride is, today, the number one medicine against dental disease. If it was used more widely by dentists, there would be far, far less dental disease in the world. In sensible percentage of solution, fluoride has been proven again and again in both research and actual practice to be virtually 100% effective against dental disease; especially when it is used in conjunction with adequate personal hygiene.

In its best application, fluoride is in a mouthrinse which any dentist can prescribe and any druggist can compound. Some already-compounded solutions are available to druggists and dentists (such as Oramedics' formula, called "Oramedics Phase III"). Using the rinse is simplicity itself; and it is *not* ingested (consumed). It is used to wash the mouth, and then it is spit out, down the drain.

Such a preparation not only fights odontosis, it has been shown to give significant "boosts" to nature's processes of healing and restoring bone and enamel.

If your dentist would like technical information, ask him to write Oramedics...or drop us a card, yourself, with the dentist's name and address. We will cheerfully prove to him, many times over, that fluoride rinse will be very beneficial to your health...and the health of his other patients. If that's what it takes to get him to give you a prescription...or sell you the rinse, himself...we'll be happy to do that.

Be prepared for resistance: No dentist likes to be told anything he doesn't already think is his own idea; especially by a patient, certainly not by another dentist —one who considers the conventional organization to be so far behind the times it is almost criminal. Besides: Once the dentist realizes that your improved hygiene and this fluoride rinse will very likely end odontosis for you and your family...what will he think about losing all that income from the disease repairs he doesn't get to make?

Still, you have to start somewhere. If you are at the point, or if you reach the point, where you need to obtain fluoride mouthrinse, there's only one way: It *must* come from someone who can prescribe it. That is either Oramedics, or your own chosen dentist. If you elect to use the latter, someone will have to convince him that it is in your best interest.

What about those clinical tests we discussed earlier? Those, of course, were the Lactobacillus Culture (saliva test) and the Navy Plaque Index (NPI). The saliva test can be done through the mail. In fact, it almost has to be done through the mail; there are very few laboratories in the U.S. who render this

130

service. You can have it done, yourself; there's nothing difficult about spitting into a specially-constructed mailing bottle, filling out a label and dropping it into the mail.

If you are on good terms with your dentist, and if he is interested in these things you're reading about, we can work with him and you both. There's no reason why you should conceal from him the fact that you want a saliva test. If he knows how to go about it, fine: His involvement is a huge plus for you, for him and for the profession of dentistry.

If he doesn't know how...or doesn't want to...we can process your test at a special research laboratory in Canton, Ohio.

The Navy Plaque Index has to be done by someone in the health care field who knows what he (or she) is doing. It isn't all that difficult, but not many dentists and even fewer assistants would know how. It simply isn't used much in conventional dentistry.

If the dentist is only interested in repairing the symptom-damage of disease past, he isn't going to go out of his way to check up on disease present or try to do anything about disease future. The N.P.I. examination would tell him absolutely nothing about current damage; it would only give you (and him) a real handle on how the disease developed, how severe it is, and what's likely to happen if you don't get busy correcting the cause of the problem.

Oramedics evaluations are simply not complete without the NPI exam. For those patients who use the through-the-mail services of Oramedics, there comes a time when they are sent the forms and instructions for the NPI exam and asked to visit a local dentist for this service.

Here again, as with the saliva test, there is a procedure you can't do for yourself without some professional help. Whether that help comes through the mail from Oramedics, or through your own chosen dentist (with Oramedics helping, if you and he wish), makes little difference to your health.

The tests *are* very, very important *provided* you are being advised (and/or treated) by a dentist who cares about your present and future oral health. In short, these tests give us an idea of where you are today, where you have to go, and how rapidly you progress toward your goal. Without them, there's no sure method of knowing whether your hygiene and dietary habits are truly effective.

How accurate are the tests? For years, patients in one Oramedics practice were told that if they followed the procedures and got passing "grades" on their saliva and NPI tests, any disease damage which developed would be treated free. Any damage, of any kind, with no question.

Nobody ever "collected" on that guarantee: Nobody who scored acceptable exam grades ever had any disease damage. Obviously: They never had any more active disease.

About foods: You should, perhaps, re-read the chapter dealing with sugar and foods in general. There is no advantage in trying to avoid sugar absolutely; you can't. Besides, you'll discover when you re-read that section that bread, for example, is worse than candy when it comes to odontosis.

Instead, think about the most reasonable approach to eating habits and your selected time for oral hygiene. Try to develop the habit of cleaning your mouth "extra" when you eat something you know is going to be "bad" for you.

Most of us spend a lot of time in one specific place each day; whether at the office, in the factory or driving a truck. Wherever you work, there's a place where you can go when "nature calls" —and that is also a place where you could stash a toothbrush and a small can of powder.

Eat what you like for lunch; just plan to return to work a few minutes earlier than usual (habit, remember?) in order to give your teeth a quick once-over.

Brushing after meals is not the sure-fire approach to oral hygiene the advertising agencies would have us believe. Brushing *well* before bedtime is always the most important. But brushing after meals *is* helpful; and if you let yourself be really truthful about it, you'll realize that it isn't as difficult as you've made it out to be.

There's one TV ad that shows a perky, smiling secretary on her way back to the office, swinging along main street; the picture of happiness and success (and several thousand dollars worth of dentistry). She flutters her eyes into the TV camera and says, "Brush after meals...? I can't!"

—Why can't she? With only 30 seconds to make their point, the Ad agency forgot to tell us why she can't slip into the "powder room" and do the job before going back to her typewriter...

The other thing you can do, at this point, is to be convinced that dental disease has got to go. Concentrate on the disease, exclusively; forget temporarily about having damages repaired. Sooner or later, you may) and probably should —want a reparative dentist to go in there and drill, fill and otherwise restore damage that's so far gone it can't be medically or naturally reversed.

That, however, is *not* the most important thing at this stage. Once you begin to combat disease effectively, there will be no further damage. The already-damaged teeth will not get worse; they may very well, in fact, get a little bit better.

You can begin planning your eventual corrective therapy by discussing disease with your dentist; by helping to make him more and more prevention-conscious. If he is interested in your health, he'll cooperate. If he is anxious to reach for the hypo and drill, you might think twice about his motives.

It comes down to this: Your own best interests are served by first eliminating disease, then correcting damage. If a dentist wants to reverse that procedure on you, he is not prevention-oriented; his priorities are more self-serving than patient-serving, and he is not doing his best *for you.*

A dentist can give you a careful examination, once your saliva count and NPI show that you have disease under control, and make out a treatment plan to correct the damages.

At that point, he and you will have many options related to what must be done first, then next, and so on. Time is no longer crucial, since the damage is not worsening. The dentist can discuss money and payment plans; timing, the whole works. He and you can have a lasting, worthwhile "partnership" which allows him to be a professional at his most competent, most rewarding performance; and which gives you as many financial and medical advantages as is possible.

It's a situation where everybody wins.

So...see your dentist. Make your home preparations by purchasing the supplies you'll need and determining how you will establish your most effective hygiene habits, and then make an appointment to talk your oral health future over with a dentist.

Show him this book, if you wish; or drop Oramedics a card and ask about our more technical booklet, "Research Advocates Oramedics," which is an overview of odontosis disease: Cause, cure and prevention.

The Oramedics medical team, its laboratories and its publications, are all available to your dentist; or to you directly, if you wish. We emphasize that dealing directly with Oramedics is an *option* available to anyone who cannot find a prevention-oriented dentist, or who prefers to "do it himself." As an option, it is just that: It is an alternative to working with a local dentist. There are advantages and disadvantages either way.

We simply want to give Americans the freedom to *choose;* and stand ready to help individuals and dentists whenever and wherever they want to enlist in the war on odontosis.

In a nutshell, that's what you can do about odontosis:

—Make some decisions...

—Make some choices...

—Make some habits and efforts...

And you're on your way. It would be good if we could *guarantee*, fairy-godfather fashion, that if you try your best you'll be totally successful.

Too much depends on you...on how good "your best" really is. We can't guarantee success if you try...

We can only guarantee failure if you don't try.

"What can I do...?"

—If you're like 98% of us, and that includes dentists, you're convinced there's *nothing* you can do.

Well, that's a lie. Why not help us help you to prove it?

Chapter Fourteen
"Whatever Happened to Doctor Nara?"

The best way to prepare you for the reception you are likely to receive in a conventional dentist's office is to tell you, in highlight form, the story of what happened to the doctor who developed Oramedics.

It's difficult to believe; but of course it is documented. It's a story that has baffled news columnists, TV news editors and everyone in the public who has ever heard it. Why on earth does organized dentistry want to destroy the man who wants to stop dental disease?

Or, as columnist Jim Fitzgerald (Detroit Free Press) put it:

"Nara received a hearing before he was suspended. It was conducted by hearing examiner Wayne Lusk of the state Department of Licensing and Regulation. He ruled that the specialty advertising charges against Nara 'failed to establish a violation.' The dentistry board voted 6-2 to suspend Nara anyway, and also voted not to use Lusk as a hearing examiner anymore."

One of the two board members voting against the 15 month suspension did so because he wanted an even longer suspension. (Unbelievable but true.)

It would be difficult to point at any one given time and say, "that's where it all began." In fact, Dr. Nara was years developing his procedures; often in advance of subsequent university research that proved he was right in many cases.

Early in his campaign to change dentistry from within, before he became 'persona non grata' to the establishment, he wrote an open letter to his colleagues. The letter was sent to thousands of dentists over the years, and it is informative enough that we should include it, here. Ask yourself one question: Why is this letter, apparently, so inflammatory when read by a conventional dentist? He wrote:

Dear Doctor:

First if you will allow me a little background. When I began to perform dental treatment in the fall of 1957, I quickly came to the realization that it was necessary to establish a healthful oral ecology before attempting to restore or replace missing teeth. It is only common sense that to fix teeth before establishing a clean healthy mouth with good gum tissue is like 'pounding sand into a rat hole.'

It is a waste of the patient's time and money to treat the results of a disease process without first straightening around the factors causing the disease. Even worse is the fact that to begin clinical repair of dental disease without insisting on proper oral hygiene makes the dentist partially responsible for keeping the patient in a neglectful frame of mind.

If the dentist does not insist on proper oral hygiene before restoring or replacing he becomes *partially responsible* for that patient's future dental disease and probable *loss* of his or her teeth. To do so is unthinkable for the socially responsible dentist.

One must recognize that to accomplish a level whereby people are really cleaning their mouths thoroughly is a very, very difficult task. After years of trial and error, making a multitude of mistakes, we finally hit upon a concept that works. This concept combines a proper psychological approach with existing clinical procedures for treating the cause of the disease along with repairing the results of the disease.

This unique combination of a new psychological delivery system along with existing clinical procedures with a few new twists is called Oramedics. In 20 years Oramedics is the first successful method that we have found that causes people to beat a path to our door.

137

Further information on Oramedics can be obtained by writing...or by speaking to me personally by calling this number...

Yours for better dental health,
/s/ Robert O. Nara, D.D.S.

Question: What is there, in that letter, that seems immoral, unethical, or any of those other "un-some-things" we hear about these days? Isn't this letter clearly a challenge to the profession; a plea for patient health, and a clear-cut offer to share these findings with other dentists?

—And that, of course, was just the beginning...

Dr. Nara's reputation for innovation —and for making a successful practice in a small, north-Michigan rural area —began to bring him invitations to lecture at meetings of fellow dentists.

He became more and more active, among other things becoming one of the youngest dentists ever elected to hold a seat in the American Dental Association House of Delegates.

His itinerary took him from coast to coast in the U.S. as well as to many foreign countries. He espoused oramedics theory and made his first most important announcements concerning preventive medical dentistry at the Federation Dentaire International in Paris, France, in 1967. His teachings were accepted by south African countries which adopted Oramedics principles nationwide and invited him to hold a position in the dental college in one country.

A growing dissatisfaction began knawing at Dr. Nara's peace of mind. Fame (of sorts) and fortune (to a degree) were his; but more and more he began to realize that his fellow dentists invited him to be keynote speaker at various dental society meetings because he could tell them how to successfully practice dentistry; could fire them with zeal and initiative to make their practices more successful.

The expression "Money Cow" began to creep into his vocabulary more and more. He realized that the dentists were listening to every word about money and success; but not paying enough attention to what he said about prevention.

He wanted to tell them how to save teeth.

They wanted him to tell them how to save time.

He wanted to tell them how to prevent disease.

They wanted to hear about how to prevent bankruptcy.

The rift began to widen; first, among the dentists who practiced near Dr. Nara's home town. His lecturing to public as well as profession was making them look bad. Dr. Nara's outspokenness often found its mark, creating resentment. The first dark cloud on the horizon was an accusation from the local dental association: Dr. Nara had a telephone yellow page listing in bold-face type instead of the standard type, like all the other dentists.

Unable to believe they were all that serious about it, Dr. Nara responded to the charge in a less-than-enthusiastic manner. After much letter writing and disputing, the charges were dropped.

Then came the highway signs: That's right, a private group, 'Citizens Action to Save Teeth', ordered highway billboards to promote oral hygiene.

Dr. Nara erected a large temporary sign in the parking lot beside his office, depicting Children's Dental Health Week.

The resentment grew; there were rumors and "rumbles" that other dentists were "out to get" Dr. Nara. In the meantime, he stepped up his campaign to inform the public about disease prevention. He was the author of numerous pamphlets on the subject; guest speaker at all kinds of civic meetings. He developed a weekly radio program which was aired throughout the area where he practiced dentistry.

Then came the infamous "advertisement" which,

ultimately, was his downfall. The yellow pages of the Houghton-Hancock (Michigan) telephone directory listed him with all of the other dentists, but with this difference: Below his name and telephone number was the message, "specializing in Oramedics —for people with teeth who want to keep them."

The dental associations brought charges against him for unethical conduct. While all of the paperwork and hearings —adjournments and re-scheduling and so on —were in progress, the state board of licensing also began to lean on him. On numerous occasions, investigators from the state board visited his office, posing as ordinary citizens, trying to find (or force) a violation of the state codes.

On one such occasion, a state investigator actually had a filling *removed* by a Lansing (Michigan state capitol) dentist, before he made the many-hundred-mile journey to the Upper Peninsula to pay a visit on Dr. Nara's office.

Official transcripts show that the investigator, lying about his identity, his home and his purpose there, came to the office complaining that the filling "fell out" while he was eating.

Dr. Nara was not in the office. In order to relieve the man's discomfort, an assistant —who, by the way, was a registered nurse —plugged the cavity with something called ZOE —zinc-oxide-eugenol. She had taken X-rays before doing this, to make sure there was nothing seriously wrong with the tooth...no infection, no problems.

ZOE is a temporary filling; the ingredients are available in any well-stocked drugstore —the co-author of this book has, himself, packed a tooth with ZOE without any assistance.

After performing this service, the nurse —at the agent's request —mounted the X-ray and gave it to him, "so he could show it to his dentist back home."

The fee for this service? —There was none! Even the official investigation report includes the information that everyone on Dr. Nara's staff treated the visitor with courtesy and friendliness. The man was told to enjoy his vacation, and to be sure he checked in with his dentist when he got back downstate.

Being treated well, and receiving free treatment —even including an X-ray —didn't stop the investigator from turning in his report. There had been a violation of the Michigan dental practice act; and charges were issued against Dr. Nara.

With charges pending against him in local, state and national dental associations; and with the state of Michigan trying to "try" him for a punishible violation, Dr. Nara *still* kept up his whirlwind schedule of lecturing and conducting seminars...and maintained a busy practice, also.

The charges and counter-charges were pending for many months. Some of the hearings and mock-trials in the dental association were conducted so unfairly that, in desperation to "get them off my back," Dr. Nara finally filed lawsuits against the associations. This eight-million-dollar suit is still pending in federal district court, after a number of hearings and "discovery procedures" in an attempt to thwart the doctor.

In one hearing, for example, the association's lawyers asked the federal judge to force Dr. Nara to turn over his patient records, so the association could examine them.

This particular hearing resulted in the ludicrous —even weird —spectacle of a battery of dental association attorneys trying to convince a judge that a dentist *is not a doctor* —that his patient records cannot be considered confidential.

The outcome of that hearing, incidentally, was not a clear-cut win or loss for either side. The associations didn't get the right to examine Dr. Nara's records... but the judge avoided making a decision regarding the status of a dentist (doctor, or no) and the confidentiality of his patient records. In a way, it's too bad there was no decision, because it leaves the Michigan state laws in limbo. There is no federal law governing dental patient records; the federal courts hold that the individual states should set their own laws on this point. In Michigan, the only applicable precedent is nearly 100 years old...dating from the days when a dentist didn't *have* to be a doctor!

When the dispute between the doctor and the associations became an outright war, he stepped up his campaign to take his case to the public. TV appearances and stories in major newspapers —Chicago, Akron, Milwaukee, Detroit to name a few —began to get the public's attention.

It got the profession's attention, too; in a way that they had never paid attention when Dr. Bob was trying to tell how *dentists* could prevent dental disease. Now he was trying to tell the *public* how to do it!

It is a matter of record that the state department of licensing and regulation "governs" the profession of dentistry through the state dental board. Who do you think sits in judgment on dentists, as members of the dental board?

You got that right...it's dentists; and they are party-line association men right down the line. When Dr. Bob's case finally came before the board, there were two charges he was facing: First, that he allowed an assistant to polish (clean) teeth —a violation in Michigan, while it is perfectly legal in 23 other states; and something that almost all dental offices are guilty of. Second: That he was advertising an illegal (un-recognized) specialty.

The yellow pages advertisement was finally coming home to haunt Dr. Bob. This "advertisement" that he specialized in Oramedics brought the state charges.

What happened?

The final step before board action, in Michigan, is a hearing before an examiner of the state's licensing and regulation department. (an administrative judge)

The results of that examination, as the transcript

unfolds, are clear-cut: Hearing examiner Wayne Lusk said that he had determined that Dr. Nara may have violated the provision of state law which says an unlicensed assistant may not perform tooth-cleaning. On the other charge, examiner Lusk's report covered every conceivable subsection and main section of the dental law, one at a time. There was no violation of subsection after subsection, therefore, said Lusk, *there had been no violation of the dental law* with respect to advertising an unrecognized specialty.

Then the board met. The decision, on the first charge, was to suspend Dr. Nara's license for three months. On the second charge: The board decided to reverse the findings of the state's own administrative judge! "No violation? Forget it!" The board found Dr. Nara guilty *anyway;* and then —incredibly —suspended his license for one full year! It made little difference, after that, but they made sure he got the full effect by making the two sentences consecutive: His license had been negated for 15 months.

Almost as an afterthought, the board next voted never again to allow the state department's man, Lusk, to be an examiner in a case involving dental licenses.

All we can indicate from the facts and records is that Dr. Nara "went down fighting" in Michigan, trying to help people save their teeth; and that one key member of the board was dissatisfied with "only" a 12-month suspension on a charge that the state's own examiner had thrown out. If there is any conclusion to be found, here, the reader will have to find it without any further help...

A look at the records of cases brought before the dental board will show that suspensions are few and far between; and that when they *do* happen, they are almost never for periods as long as a year. Usually, the suspensions are for gross violations which result in harm to patients; almost always, they are based upon complaints from the public.

Charges against Dr. Nara have been primarily

"set-ups," investigators or others they have sent in to entrap the doctor into violating some provision of the state law.

Even when the board does find a doctor guilty and suspends his license, there is a virtually-automatic appeal to the state courts. Most doctors who have grossly violated the law find themselves back in practice within a week or so: Upon filing the appeal, a "stay of suspension" is usually automatic until the appeal outcome is decided.

The courts "lost" Dr. Nara's appeal. When, after months of constant telephone calls and trips to the state capitol; after thousands of dollars in attorney fees, the court finally got around to his case, still another unusual development happened:

The office of the state attorney general filed a massive brief in the appeal court, *asking them not to hear* Dr. Nara's appeal. If, to an American citizen, it seems incredible that an appeal court would refuse to hear a request for trial...think how it seemed to Dr. Nara —a dentist, not an attorney —when he discovered that he was, suddenly, less than a citizen.

It has been nearly a year since his license was suspended. Dr. Nara still has not had a day in a real trial court! His attorneys have tried every available means to get this case tried: Nothing, so far, in either state or federal courts has been of any avail.

Once again: To an American citizen, the thought that a man can be tried, found not guilty...the decision reversed, and punishment rendered...all without ever spending a single day in a real court, with a jury and opposing lawyers...it simply is not to be believed.

But it's true. Dr. Nara has lived through this nightmare; the transcripts and records are all there, and all intact: The indisputable, provable fact is that "somebody" has pulled out all the stops: The idea is to shut this doctor up; get him out of the way, make him quit telling his story.

It didn't work. Dr. Nara continues to take his

campaign to the public. More and more, journals and broadcasters who are extremely careful to avoid "nut-cases," to stay away from controversial cases, are beginning to pick up this story. All of them are asking the same question: "Why?"

Why can't Dr. Nara's cases get into court? *Why* doesn't the national dental association make a definitive pronouncement on preventive dentistry *as a specialty*? *Why* do people —ordinary citizens from all walks of life —keep writing letters, both to Dr. Bob and to news media, extolling Oramedics as the thing which can save the dental/oral health of entire families?

Every time (rare, indeed) that the dental association faces Dr. Nara in a debate, they withdraw in shambles. On a nationally-televised talk show, recently, they sent two or three of their "big guns" to dispute Dr. Bob. It was painfully obvious to the talk show host, to the audience...and the national network audience...that the association was ducking, dodging and weaving: They cannot "win" in such a debate because, in order to "prove their case," they have to take the stand that dental disease is good for people!

It's an oversimplification, of course, but the debate could be something like this:

Dr. Bob: "All I want to do is stop dental disease, to teach dentists and people how to prevent it."

Association: "That's unethical. You shouldn't do that, Dr., and we are going to do everything we can to stop you."

Not long ago the national association spent nearly half a million dollars in a media blitz to keep people in one state from voting for "denturists." Do you know what the issue was? There was a statewide referendum which gave people the choice: Should only dentists be allowed to "fit" and "sell" dentures; or should people be able to buy dentures directly from the manufacturer?

The association threw well over $400,000 into the campaign, warning people against the "evils" of denturists. They wanted, desperately, to keep this high-paying rip-off within the trade: Dentists make literal fortunes marking up dentures by a tenfold margin.

The people in that state were not fooled: They voted for personal freedom to choose whether they could buy their dentures from a para-dentist, or —if they preferred —from a dentist.

Our point here is not whether people should be free to decide (although, obviously, we believe they should be). The point is that the association was willing to "blitz" the people in that state, throwing talent and massive sums of money into the electioneering, in order to *prevent* people from having that freedom of choice.

No Oramedics doctor would care, either way, about such a referendum. Their patients don't need dentures: Dentures are a "dirty word" to an Oramedics practitioner.

This same association which willingly spent almost a half-million (that we know about) to keep the people in one state from freedom of choice with respect to dentures...this is the same association that Dr. Nara is fighting.

If they were willing to spend so much in one state alone and on this one question alone...what lengths will they go to in order to keep Dr. Nara from telling people in *every* state that not only should they be free to buy dentures wherever they wish; they would be far, far better off if they *never* had to buy them!

In July, Dr. Nara wrote the White House:

"Dear Mr. President:

I'm sure you are unaware of it, but the fact remains that you have been lied to. In your recent contacts with the American Dental Association you have been led to believe that dentists have been diligent in keeping their prices down.

"If you would bother to investigate, you will find that the dental consumer price index is made up by monitoring fees for three services. The

146

three services are: a one-surface amalgam filling, an extraction, and a denture. A typical fee for the filling might be $8.00. For an extraction —$10.00 and for the the denture —$300.00.

"The laboratory costs to the dentist for the denture amount to less than 20%, netting the dentist after laboratory costs of over 80%. Denture fees have not been increased much by dentists in the past couple of years, the reason being the already existing wide margin of profit, and the threat of denturists." (As in the state that thumbed it's collective nose at the A.D.A.?)

—The letter continued:

"If the dental price index included gold crowns, root canals, reinforced porcelain crowns, and the like, I can assure you the dental consumer price index would be much higher than what is being falsely reported to you.

"The dental price index is just one area that is being falsely reported by the dental associations. There are others that are far more inflationary than the price index lie.

"If you are serious in your endeavor to control health costs along with other inflation, then please have a member of your staff contact me. The factors I have to relate are not opinion. I can produce valid substantiation for each of the several ways I can personally offer you to drastically reduce health care costs...

Sincerely,
/s/Robert O. Nara, D.D.S.

How much effect has Dr. Bob's campaign had, so far, on dentistry? That's a simple question, but the answer is complex. So much of the official reaction is behind the scenes we may never realize the full impact. In Michigan, however, there is indication that the dam may be cracking. Obviously, the doctor's campaign has had more effect in that state than in others: That's where it all began, and that's where the first major TV stations and newspapers began taking him seriously enough to realize that he was telling the truth: That dental disease need not be allowed free reign; and that organized dentistry *doesn't want* the people to know that.

In September of 1978 the Daily Mining Gazette in Dr. Nara's hometown, Houghton, Michigan, ran an editorial to mark the state's revision of its dental practice laws.

The editor said:

Michigan's new revised Public Health Code, which repeals the state's 39-year-old dental practice act, is more than a minor victory for Dr. Robert O. Nara of Houghton.

It would be difficult to assess how heavily influenced the code's composers were by Nara. Certainly some impact was made by his battle of more than a decade for liberalized dental laws and his license suspension for violations under the old act, which was at best vague.

In light of the new code and the questionable manner in which the old act was administered in Nara's case, we fail to see how justice can continue to be served —if, indeed, it ever was —by requiring Nara to serve the full term of his suspension.

While the new code says nothing about retroactivity, its enactment while Nara's suspension is still in effect lends a distinctly farcical appearance to the statutes under which he was prosecuted.

It's almost as if the state agencies are saying, 'We were wrong. Nara's case points that out. Let's hurry and change the law before somebody else files a multi-million dollar suit against us,' as Nara has.

To require Nara to remain on suspension is akin to going ahead with a lynching after learning no crime was committed, after all.

True, there are still rules and regulations to be promulgated under the code, but an attorney's opinion is that while a board may further liberalize some of the code's decrees, it would be difficult to make them more restrictive.

And the new code provides for delegating duties to unlicensed dental assistants, and advertising, the bases for the two charges brought against Nara.

The first charge —allowing an assistant to polish teeth —was under a regulation that apparently was never taken seriously by the profession, which may explain why the license suspension period was only three months.

The other charge against Nara —advertising an 'unrecognized specialty' —is so nebulous it could require a jury of Solomons to arrive at a definitive decision.

Nara has just completed his third month of a 12-month license suspension on the advertising charge.

We suggest the state boards of dentistry and the department of licensing and regulation redeem themselves while they are still able by restoring Nara's right to earn a living.

Of course, the boards didn't "redeem themselves" by taking the newspaper editor's advice...but the dental organizations have never been well known for taking advice from anybody...

The key thing is that, at least in Michigan, the profession is being *forced* to take another look at itself. When you couple this to such other things as a sudden rash of "preventive" articles in prestigeous dental journals, many of them "discovering" things Nara has been preaching for ten years or more, it is evidence that change is beginning to occur. Further evidence can be found in the fact that the voters of one state proved to the association that the American public isn't as stupid as those doctors wished them to be: In spite of a massive public relations "snow job," those citizens correctly figured it out: All the profession was trying to protect was its collective bank account, not the patients' health.

...What ever happened to Dr. Nara...?

He is alive and well, and he is winning...slowly... his battle to bring you, the public, the truth about dentists, dental associations, and dental disease. He is doing that by publicizing...and practicing...and teaching...an inventive oral health care "system" called Oramedics. In a sense, he has something in common with another —more famous —inventor, Thomas A. Edison.

Mr. Edison once said, "The doctor of the future will give no medicine but will interest his patients in the care of the Human Frame, in diet, and in the cause and prevention of disease."

—Right on, Tom! ...*That's* what "happened" to Dr. Nara.

Chapter Fifteen
Let's Sum It All Up...

...And, of course, that won't be particularly easy. How do you even begin summarizing a story of this magnitude, with this many ramifications?

On the attitude of "normal" dentists: Perhaps a reprint of a letter received at Oramedics headquarters tells the story as well as any other way. The dentist wrote:

I know the Oramedics program has been a highly successful program with you and other Oramedics Practitioners, but I still remain skeptical of its success in my area. I'm not sure my patients are willing to make any additional financial commitments to a program which would involve a series of treatments before the actual operative phase. Of course, you would probably rebut with the statement that 'you are just thinking negatively, and with such an attitude one's program will never succeed.'

Unfortunately, I have always been a negative thinker and find it hard to change...all my thoughts to positive ideas. Also, the financial commitment on my part to such a program would be prohibitive as to hiring an Oramedics Assistant, as I can just afford the present assistant I have who also doubles as my Receptionist. Well, so much for my alibiing...

That letter, of course, from one of the old guard; the entrenched "conventional dentists" who are trying their best to keep the status quo, to avoid innovation and change. There are a few (far too few) dentists, on the other hand, who are looking toward the modernization of dentistry with interest...even excitement.

One such dentist wrote from Las Vegas, Nevada:

> Dear Bob:
> It is interesting to hear of your progress in trying
> to make the Associations et al see what progress is.
> Our little state here, many times considered being
> ruled by dinasaur types, ruled 2 years ago that
> assistants can polish teeth —nothing disastrous
> has occured! Keep up the fight; the F.T.C. and
> your patients are obviously all for you...

It might be interesting to note, before we continue,
what this dentist referred to in mentioning the FTC:
The U.S. Government's Federal Trade Commission is
hot on the trail of the A.D.A. This is the same government agency that has been "trust-busting" for decades: Anytime they encounter a monopoly which
operates to the detriment of the public, the FTC goes
into action.

Agents of the FTC have spent many hours with
Dr. Nara, discussing the ramifications of the closed
shop as far as specialists are concerned; discussing the
obvious bad effect of the A.D.A. long-time ban on
advertising...going into price-fixing and the near-
racket-business of denture supply.

It's too long and involved to discuss here in any
detail. The point is that the FTC has decided that the
American Dental Association must be at least investi-
gated, if not indicted, for actions and attitudes which
are detrimental to the American public. That's you...
and it's a crying shame that it has been so bad for so
long that the government has to step in...and, particularly, has to step in through the door usually reserved
for illegal restraint of trade, for big-business mono-
polists.

America's dentists cry out to be treated as doctors,
as professionals...and yet their own organization is
under scrutiny as if it was a business; and a shady one,
at that.

It is a long reach from the federal government to

a rural Michigan county government, but there is a connection with respect to dentistry...and Dr. Nara.

The Houghton (Michigan) County Board of Commissioners entered this resolution into the official proceedings of February 14, 1978:

> Moved by Comm. McCormack, supported by Comm. Dwyer, that the Board authorize the Chairman to sign a letter to the State Board of Dentistry, informing them that the Houghton County Board of Commissioners take a dim view of their actions relative to the suspension of Dr. Robert O. Nara, DDS of Houghton, Michigan.

There were seven Commissioners present, and on the roll call vote, all seven voted "aye."

Over a year ago, Dr. Nara expressed his disgust with so many of his professional colleagues by writing a letter, which is a parody of what a retired "conventional dentist" might have sent to his ex-patients. The fictional "Doctor Jones" wrote this letter while basking in the sunshine of Sun City, U.S.A.:

Dear Patient of Many Years:

> For a long time now I have been meaning to tell you something. With more time on my hands these days, I am finally getting to it. I hope that you will be patient with me as this is a difficult message to convey.

> First a little background: When I graduated from dental school my mind was chucked full of mechanical knowledge. I remember the first day that you came to my office; I was so happy to see you; I was so proud of my new doctorship that the first thing I wanted to do was to get you into my dental chair and "fix something." Since dentists have always fixed or pulled bad teeth you went right along with the program. It also was advantageous to me because until I got you into that chair to fix or pull I couldn't charge you a fee.

My plan was to get on with a lot of repairing and replacing because after all I had been in school for many years and needed to catch up on all the money I lost while I was getting my education.

I really planned to go beyond the mechanical level and get into relating to you the concepts of why you had so many dental problems. But with the financial pressures of my image in the community, I never seemed to get around to sitting down and talking with you about the causes of dental problems and how to stop them from taking place.

I tried hard to get into prevention. I went to special meetings put on by the "Oramedics Evangelists." I even brought the subject up at a dental society meeting once but was admonished by my colleagues who said, "What can we say if the Public asks…'why didn't you tell me this *before?*' "

An honest answer would have exposed the profession, so obviously I couldn't do that.

The days moved into weeks, weeks into months, and months into years. Oh, sure, I did tell my hygienist who I kept on half-hour appointments to tell you to floss, but none of us ever got around to telling you WHY.

Because you didn't know why, I can understand why you seldom bothered to "clean between" your teeth or brush any better than you ever did, although most of my life I blamed *you* for causing your own dental disease.

With all of this time on my hands these days between shuffleboard and pinochle, I have figured out that the real reason that you suffered so much dental disease was that I never took the time to explain the exact *cause* and relate to you *why* certain things must be done to prevent further trouble.

In the first line of this letter I said that for a

long time I have been meaning to tell you something. That something is: All of the things that I fixed for you...for money...all could have been prevented in the first place!

Your friend,
Dr. Jones (retired)
Sun City

That letter, of course, is fictional; but it might very well have been written by a number of retired dentists. One dentist, for example, bragged about never having owned an X-ray machine: He was honored at a meeting of the dental association in his semi-retirement. Typical of the "trade?" The man, by his own admission, had removed three million teeth in his career.

The fictional "Dr. Jones" of the above letter also might well have been a California dentist...who, fortunately, didn't get away with doing the things "Dr. Jones" talks about in his letter. The California dentist was sued —successfully —by patients who charged him with malpractice, for treating the symptoms of a preventable disease without doing anything about the disease itself.

If we could get enough Americans to slap malpractice suits, on every dentist in America, we'd change the face of dentistry overnight.

That, obviously, isn't going to happen.

And so we will have to keep slugging it out, one day at a time and one case at a time, until American Dentistry joins the twentieth century. It's about time: We are perilously near the 21st century already!

Dentistry will manage to hang on to its old ways of doing things for decades, unless the American Public becomes informed and demands change. As it stands, so few are aware that anything can really be done about dental disease, they simply don't care. That "don't care" attitude is nurtured and nourished by the profession itself; because for obvious reasons they don't dare tell the whole truth, all at once.

It isn't a question of money, either. The American Public avoids dentists, but it's more because they believe dental disease and all of its consequences to be inevitable. Why bother to "keep up" your teeth when you will lose them all, anyway? Many people just wait until an aching tooth sends them to an obliging dentist, who yanks it out...cheap.

The way people spend money on health care shows an amazing lop-sidedness toward the medical doctor instead of the dental doctor; toward the health of the body...but not the mouth.

If that were the only comparison, it would be bad enough. But consider this: The same American Public spends more on jewelry than on dental health care; it spends half again as much on cosmetics than on dental health care. Think that's bad? People spend more than twice as much on tobacco than on dental health...and more than *three times* as much on liquor!

How many remember the cartoon character, "Pogo?" In his immortal words: "We have met the enemy, and he is us."

The enemy is the profession of organized dentistry, which wants to avoid anything that smacks of genuine preventive medical dentistry. They are locked into the drill, spit and fill; the denture-oriented trade, the cheap extractions. The industry "behind" dentistry —many billions of dollars a year —survives *because* of dental disease; not in spite of it.

The enemy is also "us" —the American public who has swallowed the Big Lie; hook, line and sinker. While we were all waiting for the dental profession to lead the way, we got lost at the pass.

The enemy is also the government; and mostly the various state governments, with their antiquated health laws, their profession-serving boards and regulatory agencies. It's too much to hope for, that county and state level legislators could turn out health laws without "a little help" from the health care professions involved. Is it any wonder that laws written by dentists, for dentists, are not exactly in the best interests of the public they are really meant to serve and protect?

But let's bring it back to frame one; to ground zero. *Who* is the enemy?

—The enemy is *odontosis*; and it is a disease; a preventible disease. It is caused by *germs.* The germs can be avoided, counteracted, killed.

There are medical tests to determine the extent of the disease; there are medical and hygenic approaches which will destroy the disease process.

The approach to prevention is, most properly, that of enlightened patient in partnership with an innovative doctor. Without the innovative doctor, the enlightened patient will have to work a little harder; assume a bit more responsibility. But it *can* be done.

We can enlighten patients. You, reading this, are an enlightened patient. We can ever continue to recruit preventive dentists; "real doctors," converts from the "profession" of organized dentistry.

We can slug it out with the states and the associations; we can try to get the federal government more deeply involved. These steps are time consuming, and the results are painfully slow.

We *are* making more headway among the health-conscious sector of the American public. To these people, natural healing is easily-understood. The cleansing, rejuvenating processes of whole-body health have been their "thing" for years; as they learn that Mother Nature didn't stop with her health-orientation at the limits of the mouth, such people become converts...and become healthy.

We have begun working with others in the health care field; even with those only loosely related to health care. These people range all the way from school nurses to teachers, from chiropractors to paramedics. Such health professionals are usually more easily convinced than dentists...and they are proving surprisingly effective. Perhaps their effectiveness is because they are at the point of contact: In these health professions, they meet the American public in a one-on-one basis, where health is the main topic of discussion.

We will continue to work toward the elimination of odontosis; toward the re-structuring of the dental profession and toward the goal of bringing dental/oral health into the whole-body health field; perhaps very much as Thomas Edison remarked, as we quoted earlier.

Ultimately, whatever we do; on any scale, must come down to the level of person to person if it is to be of any benefit to *you*. While Oramedics is working to bring dental health into the present, what will you be doing about your personal oral health?

This book was written with individuals in mind. If it were written for only one or two people, it would be important. If it were written only for *you*, it would be important. —How important? Well...how important is your health...your appearance...your mental and emotional well-being...your nourishment? How important is retaining (or losing) ten years of your life span?

In other words...you've learned more about odontosis than many *dentists* know, today. You've had an opportunity to look at what's wrong with the profession. You've been invited to become part of the solution to the problem.

The oral health of the future can be yours, right now. You can start today: There's enough information in this book to send you on your way. There's help, if you need it, available from Oramedics.

All that's really needed is for you to make a *decision* that you want to enjoy freedom from dental disease; and then make a *commitment* to yourself that you'll do whatever is necessary to achieve it.

You may have to argue with your dentist, but

158

that won't hurt you...or him, for that matter.

You may have to change your habit patterns a little bit; but you've changed habits before when you wanted something...you can do it again, when the benefits are this attractive.

Or...you can put this book aside and, after a few days pass, simply forget about it. From time to time, you might think of it as "something you mean to do."

If that's the case, we can give you some advice to use "until you get around to taking care of your health:"

...Brush after meals, use floss, avoid sweets, and see your dentist twice a year.

It won't help you very much, but maybe —just maybe —it's better than nothing at all. And it will help your dentist...a whole lot. He has to maintain his income, and there's only one way he can do that...

...at your expense. After all, that's how he makes his money —by the mouthful.

Because incentive is vital to your achievement of oral health, we are including these (unsolicited) letters which are typical of many in our files. These came from people just like you, and they tell the story of what Oramedics methods can do...

Dear Dr. Bob:

As you know, I've been a faithful and satisfied patient of yours for roughly seventeen years. I was fortunate to have parents who wanted to provide me with good dental care; however, we didn't realize how long lasting the effects of the preventive program were to be.

As I was growing up, I followed the steps of your preventive program. I used the disclosing tablets, brushed and flossed my teeth, and took the saliva tests. All of the information which I was using to keep my teeth clean, I took for granted because I thought other dentists all across the country were helping their patients in the same way. As I grew older, I realized that only a few dentists were showing their patients how to keep their teeth free from dental disease.

Today, I had a new experience with the Oramedics program. I came to your office for my six-months checkup and I was given the opportunity to clean and polish my teeth. With a few simple directions and the use of a Floxite® mirror, I was able to clean and polish my own teeth. Since I had been keeping my teeth clean for years, it was a logical step for me to do my own cleaning and polishing. By putting polish on my teeth and then using Clean-Between, I was also able to polish the spaces between my teeth. Not only did I get my teeth "squeaky clean," but I had fun while I was doing it. How many people can say they enjoy going to their dentists?

You then examined my teeth and gums and found them to be in excellent condition. As part of the Oramedics program, I did not have to pay any charges for the checkup because my mouth was free from dental disease. How many people can say they go to their dentists free of charge?

The suspension of your license for fifteen months not only violated your rights, but it violated mine also. I was deprived of the opportunity to choose the type of dental care which was best for me. I will continue to choose the Oramedics approach to dental care because it is sensible, cost effective, and it results in healthy teeth and gums.

Sincerely,
Linda L. Kesti
77 Second Street
South Range, MI
August 27, 1979

Dear Dr. Bob:

Thank you! I can't say enough about home gum care using the WaterPik® device and amazing new Oramedics WaterTip. Instead of agony, expense and tooth loss I now enjoy healthy gums, and in just nine days after beginning your methods.

Last fall my dentist told me I (once again) had severe gum disease and would require periodontal surgery. Having gone through two extensive and painful sessions of this some 8 or 9 years ago, being ill for days afterward and spending far too much money, I told my dentist I would rather lose all of my teeth than go through that again. He said I would most certainly lose my teeth if I didn't accept the proposed referral and have gum surgery done.

Earlier this year I heard about Oramedics and on June 12 I began the program. Following your simple instructions and using the lighted mirror, I found the WaterTip simple to master, and began using it once daily.

At first, some sort of creamy-colored stuff came out of the pockets, but that disappeared on the 3rd day. By the 4th day, the pockets had tightened so much I could not insert the WaterTip into the pockets. (I also located a couple of other pockets I hadn't known about, or seen, simply by going around each tooth with the Tip.

Today (June 21, 1979) is the 9th day of the program. All of the pockets are closed and tight; my gums are a healthy-looking pink, and there is no more soreness or discomfort. Now that I have no soreness, I recall that before my gums were very sensitve where there were pockets and I had unconsciously learned to "favor" those teeth in chewing.

I've also noticed an increase in saliva. Sitting as I am now, there's enough to bathe upper and lower teeth without constant evacuation. Do you think that my healing gums have triggered nature's healing process? From my Oramedics materials, I know the value of adequate saliva.

I'm amazed and pleased at the results in such short order. The WaterTip is so easy to use and leaves the mouth feeling so refreshed. How great it is to arise each morning without my mouth tasting like the bottom of a bird cage!

Sincerely yours,
Eldon Angus

Dear Dr. Nara:

You already know some of my oral health background, so I won't elaborate. I'm from a working-class family; both of my parents had dentures before 45 years of age. None of the five children were persuaded to do anything about oral health and as a result, by the time (at 18) when the Navy's dentists first looked at my mouth, it was a nightmare.

The classic example is a right upper molar which the dentist completely hollowed out —it's a shell —and filled with a temporary filling so he could play golf that afternoon. He had no way of knowing that my (Marine) division was going to play "get on a boat and go soldiering" the next morning.

Almost 20 years later that filling came out. By then I'd lost two other beneficial teeth: Perhaps unusually lucky, at my age and ignorance, to have suffered so little loss. However, every one of my teeth had some kind of problem, whether cavity damage or advancing gum disease.

It was during this period that I was introduced to Oramedics through the mail. Of course I was a skeptic initially: What could I do for myself that neither nature or doctors had done for me in over 20 years? I was even more suspicious because of the low cost: Only $24 for initial testing and consultation; maybe $30 to $40 for materials...? "Come on," I said; "Who does this dentist think he's kidding?"

But it was also the low cost that induced me to try it on a virtual "what have I got to lose" basis. I'd just recovered from an abscess formed on that hollow tooth —my cheek stuck out like a golf ball —and I was determined not to go through the agony and nausea of another one of those!

I did what Oramedics told me to do: It's that simple. I learned a whole new realm of self-health maintenance. You not only told me to "bake a cake," you gave me the recipe.

I filled that tooth, following your instructions, using eugenol and Cavit® filling material. I took care of the

164

gum disease problems with a WaterPik® and special tip. I polished my teeth and learned how to **keep** them clean.

All of that was nearly a year ago, now. I suppose a dentist would think my filling was amateurish, but it's holding. A year without toothache! A year of eating what I please, when I want to! A year of steadily-growing conviction that I will never again have "bad teeth" —and maybe not even bad breath!

Frequently people in religious orders work with folks in social and economic poverty. To such people, dentistry is a thing available only to the wealthy: The "ordinary" citizen has no alternative to pain, discomfort and ultimate tooth loss...with all of the whole-body disorders such an oral condition engenders over a lifetime.

The Oramedics "way" could be a God-send to such folks —it was to me —and all I can do is look forward to the day when government and social agencies finally recognize the real value of your contributions, instead of trying to block this desperately-needed progress.

Had I grown up involved with a preventive practice; if my family had been orally aware, perhaps your methods would have guaranteed I'd never never have wholesale dental health problems. But: How many people are there, like me, who became adults without benefit of any real dental attention, preventive or conventional? To us folks, "dentistry" means "pull teeth," and then only when the pain is so bad it becomes worth the expense.

Please, Dr. Nara: When "ordinary" people ask you if Oramedics can help **them**, after a lifetime of abuse and oral neglect...Tell them **yes!** Tell them my story, if it helps. Tell them ordinary people can learn not only how to prevent dental problems by themselves; they can also learn how to take care of even **severe** damage already present —**without a dentist!**

I realize your professional ethics frown on telling folks to **avoid** doctors. But there are probably millions of people who, for whatever reason, simply **can't afford** typical dental care. What, or who, offers any hope to such people?

165

"See your dentist twice a year...?" —For folks like me, seeing a dentist twice in a lifetime is more like it! It is obscene to offer these millions only one choice: See a dentist...or suffer.

Oramedics works! It is a reasonable, effective approach as an alternative to the choice between all or nothing at all. If there is any way I can be of help in furthering your work —and God knows how important it is —please let me help.

Sincerely,
Paul, BSG
Brotherhood of St. Gregory

ORAMEDICS INTERNATIONAL PRESS was established in 1978 by Oramedics International when it became apparent that most U.S. publishing houses avoid books which are either controversial or of relatively lesser commercial value, no matter how beneficial publication would be as a contribution to mankind.

Since its inception O.I. Press has published books and manuals which have established their value both in benefits to those who have read them and in the marketplace: People buy them.

A partial list of publications:

Money By The Mouthful

An expose of the dental profession with information about dental disease and its prevention.

How To Become Dentally Self-Sufficient

A lay person's "cookbook" of self-administered dental care—How to avoid disease and apply "first aid" to problems caused by prior disease. Save thousands of dollars in dentist bills.

The 180° Theory

How to become mentally self-sufficient; a self-help guide to coping with life and developing lasting peace of mind.

Get Rich Hell, Get Well!

A step-by-step method of becoming financially independent. *Not* just another get-rich-quick scheme (get rich, hell!) —this book helps the reader achieve financial health...to get "well."

What Makes Johnny Run

An overview of the psychology of individual dentists and of organized dentistry as a whole.

Feelings: Having an Encounter With Yourself

The publication which prompted *The 180° Theory*; considered by many an essential companion to *The 180° Theory:* A workbook-format to help develop personal mental and emotional growth.

*The Psychology of Credit and Collections
in Dental Practice*

How to extend credit and collect payment easily without creating ill-will; written for dentists, beneficial to many professions.

*Building Positive Mental Attitude
in Dental Practice*

A guide to coping with the emotional stress of this mentally-damaging profession.

Research Advocates Oramedics

A concise, but thorough, analysis of dental disease (odontosis) and Oramedics International's preventive approaches. Includes all known applicable research through early 1979. All statements documented in complete bibliography.

Applied Oramedics for Health Care Professionals

A step-by-step method for any member of the health care field to help patients and clients overcome and prevent dental disease (odontosis).

Changing Idealism Into Realism

The "Big Book" of Oramedics (for dentists): How to establish and maintain a preventive dental practice. Its 3-ring binder format allows constant updates and revisions. (Sold only upon approval of Oramedics International.)

* * *

Numerous brochures and pamphlets are available for use by dentists and the public, covering almost any topic in preventive (medical and self-help) dentistry; oral health care.

* * *

SOON TO COME: *Wounded Women;* a study of women emotionally crippled, victimized by bad marriages. Self-help guide to discovering the problems (and causes) in a damaging marriage; how to recover your own personality and regain emotional health.

* * *

A postcard to Oramedics International Press, 200 East Montezuma Ave., Houghton, MI 49931, will bring an up-to-date list of titles in print and current price information. *If you can't find the title you want in your bookstore* it can be ordered direct from O.I. Press.

YES...SEND _____ EVALUATIONS, ONE FOR EACH INDIVIDUAL LISTED:

NAME	AGE	Condition of teeth now
		good bad avg.
_____	____	( ) ( ) ( )
_____	____	( ) ( ) ( )
_____	____	( ) ( ) ( )
_____	____	( ) ( ) ( )
_____	____	( ) ( ) ( )

USE ADDITIONAL SHEET TO LIST OTHERS

SEND TO:

Name _____

Address _____ ZIP _____

Please enclose check or money order:

Individual rate—$24.00

Family rate— $24.00 for first family member,
$20.00 for each additional member

MAIL THIS CARD TO:

ORAMEDICS INTERNATIONAL
200 East Montezuma Avenue
Houghton, Michigan 49931

Place order, check and any other information in envelope and mail today!

169